Kurth, Burton O

Milton and Christian heroism; Biblical epic themes and forms in seventeenth-century England, by Burton O. Kurth. Hamden, Conn., Archon Books, 1966.

152 p. 22 cm

"First published 1959 ... reprinted ... in an unaltered and unabridged edition."

Bibliography: p. 159–162.

1. Milton, John, 1608–1674—Religion and ethics. 2. English literature—Early modern (to 1700)—Hist. & crit. 3. Heroes in literature. 4. Bible in literature. I. Title.

PR3592.R4K8 1966   821.4   66–11605

MILTON AND CHRISTIAN
HEROISM

MILTON AND CHRISTIAN HEROISM

*Biblical Epic Themes and Forms
in Seventeenth-Century England*

By Burton O. Kurth

ARCHON BOOKS
HAMDEN, CONNECTICUT
1966

FIRST PUBLSHED 1959
UNIVERSITY OF CALIFORNIA PUBLICATIONS
ENGLISH STUDIES: 20

REPRINTED 1966 WITH PERMISSION
IN AN UNALTERED AND UNABRIDGED EDITION

LIBRARY OF CONGRESS CATALOG CARD NUMBER: 66-14605
PRINTED IN THE UNITED STATES OF AMERICA

TO MY FATHER AND MOTHER

ACKNOWLEDGMENTS

FOR encouragement and help in preparing this study, I am most deeply indebted to Professor Josephine Miles of the University of California, Berkeley, under whose patient and skillful direction the work first emerged as a doctoral dissertation, and whose subsequent suggestions have been invaluable. I also wish to pay my respects to the memory of the late Professor George R. Potter of the University of California, Berkeley, under whose kindly and tolerant supervision I began to wrestle with the materials which eventually pointed to Milton and this subject. Of the many others whose interest and knowledge influenced the shaping of this work, I should like to thank in particular Professor Ernest L. Tuveson, and for the original stimulation to look into the Renaissance materials, the late Professor G. G. Sedgewick of the University of British Columbia and Professor Sears Jayne. For the latest assistance in preparing this text for publication, my thanks to Miss Genevieve Rogers of the University of California Press, whose judicious use of the red pencil indicated that not all was clear, or significant, or obvious. For any "vast profundity obscure" which remains I accept full responsibility.

B. O. K.

CONTENTS

INTRODUCTION

IN HIS provocative study of the Romantic hero, W. H. Auden quite rightly suggests that analysis of "the kinds of individuals which writers in various periods have chosen for their heroes often provides a useful clue to the attitudes and preoccupations of each age, for a man's interest always centers, consciously or unconsciously, round what seems to him the most important and still unsolved problem."[1] For the seventeenth century one of the main preoccupations was the religious problem of man's relation to God and the universe, the solution of which was not necessarily a matter of justifying man's ways only. In this case it is not the preoccupation which needs clarification, but the pattern of heroism which was developed as part of the attempt to answer the problem.

The phrase "Christian hero" is a familiar one, yet is often regarded simply as a rather stereotyped personification of the "ideal" or "virtuous" Christian. For Milton, and for most seventeenth-century Protestants, this would be a very imperfect and incomplete view. The Christian hero was conceived as aspiring to the perfection of his ideal and model, Christ, but in his nature he was still fallen man and hence imperfect. He had to contend with his own limitations as well as with the forces of evil in the world. The course of his warfare with evil was by no means always marked with success, nor was he always vouchsafed that beatific vision of ultimate soul's peace and sanctification toward which he struggled. His way, like that of Bunyan's Christian, was uncertain and beset with traps and snares into which his own nature might lead him. Heroism, in short, was hard work, and the rewards lay primarily in the hero's strengthened faith and in his ability to persevere, rather than in rest and enjoyment of the fruits of this world. Further-

---

[1] For notes to the Introduction see page 143.

more, the Christian hero had to beware of taking pride in his exceptional faith and to avoid the snare of assuming worldly praise or benefits to be a just measure of his heroism.

If Christian heroism was hard and fraught with suffering, it had also its comforting and sustaining aspects. Unlike the Romantic hero, whose special mark was often his loneliness and unhappiness, the seventeenth-century Christian hero was not necessarily viewed as eccentric or isolated. Because the struggle took place within the individual, yet with consequences in the world around him, he tended to see himself as the microcosm within which was played in small the cosmic drama of the warfare between good and evil, between Christ and Satan. He could project his own limited heroic action, as it were, upon the vast cyclorama of the macrocosm, the universe itself, and see himself not alone in time but in the company of all the saints and martyrs of universal history.

The concept of the Christian hero as an actor in the cosmic drama was a vital part of seventeenth-century thought, but it has not been sufficiently recognized as a significant feature of Milton's major works. This study seeks to demonstrate the way in which this concept of heroism was adapted to the requirements of a literary genre by those English poets in the first half of the seventeenth century who conscientiously aspired to write a specifically Christian epic, and who turned to the Bible for their subject matter. The minor literary works of any period usually deserve to be regarded as minor because they have little or no intrinsic merit. They may, however, be worth dusting off if they throw some light on works of major importance. The search for sources, analogues, influences, parallels, and correspondences has long been an engrossing one in Milton scholarship, for the rich texture of ideas in Milton's works has required extensive reconstruction of his intellectual milieu. Such an approach is especially necessary in the present age, which has compounded its own complexities in other areas of thought and has forgotten much that was considered primary in a more consciously Christian society.

The search has generally been fruitful, enriching our knowledge of the period, if not always of Milton or his works. The assessment and interpretation of this knowledge, however, has not always yielded that harmonious vision toward which all right-thinking scholars aspire. Indeed, as one forthright critic of Milton scholarship has recently pointed out,[2] there are now so many disparate views and opinions that reconciliation of most or all of them has become almost impossible. It might seem presumptuous to add a further study involving some quite minor seventeenth-century works and their relationship to Milton's major and minor epics; yet this book is offered with the hope that the concepts and traditions discussed herein may help a little to bring the ultimate vision into focus.

The minor works under consideration here were nearly all attempts to find a suitably exalted form for Biblical materials, and conversely, because of the widespread admiration for classical epic models, to find Biblical subjects and themes best suited to heroic poetry. A number of compromises had to take place. The traditional nature of Biblical materials prevented any radical transmutation into classical form, and the Renaissance concept of heroic poetry was so general and eclectic that poets continued to use traditional devotional and allegorical forms of expression for Christian themes in combination with classical forms. The main problem was to find an adjustment that would preserve the Christian values within a framework of the religious view of the world, yet allow these values to be portrayed in active heroic terms. A concept of heroic action distinct from that of the pagan classics was therefore necessary. The Christian hero had to be one who exemplified both the active worldly virtues and the contemplative spiritual ideals.

Although it is often necessary to make fine distinctions between Catholic and Protestant, and between Anglican and Puritan, such distinctions are not always easy to maintain in consideration of broad and traditional Christian concepts. This study attempts to distinguish the Protestant characteristics from those of traditional Catholicism primarily in terms of the Protestant concern with the literal sufficiency of the Bible as the divinely appointed manual of instruction for the individual soul. The Protestant emphasis tended to fall more directly upon the relationship between the Biblical stories and the experience of the wayfaring, warfaring Christian. Most Catholics and Protestants, however, held in common the Christian view of universal history as set forth in such patristic works as Augustine's *City of God*. In their concept of the cosmic drama and of the course of universal history, Vida and Milton worked fundamentally in the same tradition.

The distinction between Anglican and Puritan similarly tends to disappear in relation to these broad themes and concepts. William Haller is inclined to view the theme of temptation, struggle, and triumph as particularly Puritan, and demonstrates convincingly the dominance of the theme in the sermons, tracts, and pamphlets of the Puritan preachers.[3] But, as this study attempts to show, the theme is dominant also in the Biblical narrative poems, and only a few of the poets can be called Puritan in an absolute sense. Most of them belonged, nominally at least, to the Established Church, and in the Civil War adhered to the Royalist cause. Even such sober and "Puritanical" poets as Peyton and Quarles had no affiliation with the Puritan sects. At best it can be said that Protestantism in England in the first half of the century held both traditional Christian concepts and radical ideals of reformation in an uneasy and often surprising variety of combinations.

In their search for heroic materials and themes, the Biblical narrative poets explored three main Scriptural subject matters: the hexameral,[4] the Old Testament, and the New Testament. In each they made use of the rich store of traditional commentary and exegesis that had become associated with these subjects; this extra-Biblical material in turn helped to determine the form and design of their heroic treatments. In the analysis of these areas of subject matter, it is shown that separately none of them yielded a wholly successful epic design, but that when used together within the larger vision of the cosmic drama and the course of universal history, they provided the main themes and concepts which Milton was to combine in a truly comprehensive Christian epic. In this sense it is demonstrable that Milton was as much the culmination of an English tradition of sacred heroic poetry as of the more general Renaissance and Continental aspirations to write the ideal Christian epic.

CHAPTER I

THIS SUBJECT FOR HEROIC SONG

IN THE prologue to Book IX of *Paradise Lost,* Milton gave recognition to the traditional view of the Fall as a profound tragedy, a catastrophe second to none in the history of man: "I now must change/ Those Notes to Tragic" (5–6). Yet a few lines later he qualified the statement with a return to the epic view: "Sad task, yet argument/ Not less but more Heroic than the wrath/ Of stern *Achilles* ..." (13–15). Some twenty lines later, he made more explicit what he meant by "Heroic": "the better fortitude/ Of Patience and Heroic Martyrdom/ Unsung ..." (31–33). The Fall, then, was tragic, but the subsequent actions of Adam and Eve, and of mankind, could be viewed as aspects of a concept of heroism familiar to Milton's contemporaries. Both the suffering of the tragic hero and the lofty passions of the classical epic hero could be regarded as special or extraordinary kinds of human experience. But the heroism of faith and endurance in the great warfare between good and evil, a struggle taking place in both the world and the souls of men, transcended these special heroisms. Not only were the consequences of universal significance, but also each individual Christian was potentially a hero in the greatest of epic contests. By keeping the human action at the center of his design, Milton succeeded in dramatizing the concept that the struggle with evil could be carried on in the human realm by man himself as heroic protagonist in the larger plan of Eternal Providence to bring good out of evil.

Milton broke with the harsher Calvinistic insistence upon the absolute depravity of human nature after the Fall, and stressed the potentiality, though limited, of regeneration in the individual human being. The immediate results of the Fall were

catastrophic, but if Providence was to bring greater good out
of this apparent victory for evil, the Fall should be viewed as
the beginning of a larger heroic action rather than as the end
of a tragedy. It was important, therefore, that Milton portray
Adam and Eve as repentant and submissive in Books X and
XI, for, though their reason was clouded and imperfect as a
result of the Fall, they had begun to grasp the full meaning of
their act in relation to the larger issues of good and evil. It is
on the basis of their bewildered but sincerely repentant prayers
that the Son intercedes with God for mercy and grace:

> See Father, what first fruits on Earth are sprung
> From thy implanted Grace in Man, these Sighs
> And Prayers, which in this Golden Censer, mixt
> With Incense, I thy Priest before thee bring,
> Fruits of more pleasing savour from thy seed
> Sown with contrition in his heart, than those
> Which his own hand manuring all the Trees
> Of Paradise could have produc't, ere fall'n
> From Innocence.
>
> (XI, 22–30)

Milton thus showed the relationship of two main elements
in his design: the workings of Eternal Providence, and the
qualities and conditions central to the concept of Christian
heroism. Man, once fallen, must taste the bitter fruit of sin and
suffering, must experience the assaults of evil upon his remaining virtue. Yet trial and suffering are to be regarded not only
as just punishment for sin but also as the means by which man
can acquire greater wisdom and spiritual understanding, and
prove himself worthy of redemption. The final instructions of
Michael in Book XII are that Adam must learn to measure
"this transient World, the Race of Time" (554) and to act with
Faith, Virtue, Patience, Temperance, and Love. If this is done,
Michael promises Adam, and man, "A Paradise within thee,

happier far" (587). Milton's emphasis upon man's free will is
of the utmost importance to the concept of Christian heroism,
because it makes clear that man has the choice of going two
ways, and that choice and trial are essential to the process of
regeneration. Before Christ came to restore the balance and
make the full Atonement which was beyond the power of
fallen man, the human race could only struggle with evil im-
perfectly. After the Redemption, man can attain to salvation
through faith and the merits imputed to man by Christ's sacrifice. In the cosmic or universal perspective, however, man must
continue his struggle with evil until the Last Judgment, and on
the model of his supreme Hero, Christ, endeavor to bring good
out of evil.

Milton undoubtedly assumed that his readers comprehended
these fundamental Christian principles concerning man's part
in universal history and his relationship to Christ as the central
figure in the divine historical process. The long tradition of
typological interpretation[1] in the commentaries and exegesis
had firmly established the concept of certain Biblical figures
as types foreshadowing Christ; just as fundamental was the
concept that the individual Christian could follow the pattern
of Christ's heroism within the bounds of human limitation,
that is, achieve exaltation through humiliation and suffering
in the cause of good. It is no longer possible to view Milton
as a somewhat eccentric and isolated individual in relation to
the thought of his contemporaries. Neither is it possible to set
him down simply as an extreme Puritan, cut off by rigid doc-
trines and personal heresies from the intellectual wealth of the
long Christian tradition. Recognizing that Milton drew widely
upon the resources of traditional Christian thought and commentary, we need to look more closely at the way in which
Milton utilized these materials in working out the structural

---

[1] For notes to chapter i see page 143.

problems posed by the epic genre, and undertook to give these fundamental Christian ideals and concepts coherent expression for the first time in a unified epic form. For a more complete understanding of these problems, we need to go back to the point where the poets of Protestant England began to aspire to the ideal of the Biblical epic, and to examine the various ways in which they attempted to realize this ideal. It will become clear that mere imitation of Homer or Virgil could not provide a form adequate to meet the special problems posed by a Biblical subject, and that poets continued to employ the traditional types and forms of Christian material, such as hexameral commentary and allegorical dramas of the soul, in combination with classical heroic elements.

Milton's predecessors in the genre of the Biblical epic began with little more than a general admiration of heroic poetry as the noblest kind and a profound reverence for the Bible as the repository of the sublimest materials. This admiration and reverence combined to produce a genuine enthusiasm for the concept of the Biblical epic as the ideal heroic poem. Enthusiasm and noble aspirations, however, were one thing; the practical matter of creating the Biblical epic was another. Several major problems of subject matter and form made the realization of the ideal extremely difficult; these eventually were solved only when their elements were seen to be related within a specifically Christian epic design rather than a design that merely imitated the classical epic. First, there was the lack of any clear sense of what the Biblical heroic poem should ideally be, and hence the need to develop a design that would satisfy the desire for both sublime subject matter and proper epic form. Second, directly related to the first, was the problem of finding a suitable way of adjusting Biblical materials to epic forms without yielding to the strong attraction of the conventional and traditional modes of treating these materials. Third was the problem of the epic hero. The Christian hero could be like the classical hero in some respects, but he had to be much more, and in certain ways quite different, if he could properly be called Christian. There was also the historical and theological question whether Biblical personages from the Old Testament could qualify as examples of Christian heroism. A comprehensive design had to be developed to resolve all these issues. Compromise and adjustment had to take place, and the works themselves are the best evidence of the experiments which culminated in Milton's full-fledged sacred epic.

The Biblical narrative poetry of the first half of the seventeenth century was in part the result of a strong interest in divine poetry which had begun to develop in the latter half of the sixteenth century.[2] This divine poetry was intended primarily to provide instruction in the fundamental Christian truths, particularly those drawn directly from the Bible. Such didactic poetry usually took the traditional forms of paraphrase, devotional commentary, or moral discourse. Where the text of the Bible was involved, as in the metrical paraphrases, the zeal of the early reformers had been accompanied by a rigid insistence upon the literal sufficiency of the Word of God that held in check any desire to explore the literary possibilities of the sacred materials. Before the narrative poets could aspire to the writing of sacred heroic poems, the problem of the literary treatment of the Scriptures had to be solved. The question was whether the Biblical text could be adapted freely enough to fit a pattern modeled on that of classical heroic poetry. It is evident, however, that the Protestant concern for the Bible as a theological and devotional document actually helped to further an interest in its literary resources.

Sidney, in the *Apologie for Poesie,* argued convincingly that David's Psalms were poetry, and proclaimed his enthusiasm for the sublime effects of such "heavenlie poesie."[3] By his calm and undogmatic assertion that a "little deeper" look into the Bible in the spirit of quiet judgment would reveal the poetry, Sidney indicated that it was personal experience and not ancient authority which should determine the reader's response.[4] This view helped to encourage a freer appreciation of the beauty and sublimity of the Bible, and neatly circumvented the arguments of Puritans like Gosson whose attacks upon poetry as a whole were based upon such authorities as Plato. Furthermore, Sidney's central definition of poetry was immediately followed by the unequivocal declaration that the highest type of poetry was that which figured forth Divine Perfection, and his examples were first and foremost those of the Bible: "The chiefe both in antiquitie and excellencie were they that did imitate the inconceivable excellencies of GOD. Such were *David* in his Psalms, *Salomon* in his song of Songs, in his Ecclesiastes, and Proverbs, *Moses* and *Debora* in theyr Hymnes, and the writer of *Job*."[5] By the beginning of the seventeenth century, there was a growing appreciation of the Bible as a rich source of elevated subjects and themes admirably suited to heroic treatment.

It is not surprising that Biblical narrative poetry should move toward a heroic form modeled on that of the classical epics of Homer and Virgil. These epics, though pagan, had long been considered morally edifying so far as they exalted the virtues, revealed the dangers of moral weakness or lack of self-control, and provided models of heroism that could be translated into modern terms. There had not been developed, however, a theory of epic poetry that would give direction for a heroic poem utilizing Biblical materials. English critical writings as exemplified by Sidney and Puttenham did little more than exalt the heroic genre and describe the epic as setting forth in sublime form the noble actions of worthy examples from history. In Sidney's words, "But if anything be already said in the defence of sweet poetry, all concurreth to the maintaining the heroical, which is not only a kind, but the best and most accomplished kind of poetry. For, as the image of each action stirreth and instructeth the mind, so the lofty image of such worthies most inflameth the mind with desire to be worthy, and informs with counsel how to be worthy."[6] The English models for heroic poetry were such radically different works as Spenser's *Faerie Queene,* Sylvester's translation of Du Bartas's *Divine Weekes* and *Judith,* or the patriotic historical epics, Daniel's *Civil Wars* and Drayton's *The Barons' Wars* and *Polyolbion.* The epic, apparently, was to be distinguished chiefly by its magnitude and sublimity, and by its nobility of theme and subject. It was generally agreed, also, that the primary purpose of the epic was didactic: it should illuminate the problems and conditions of the reader's own time. In the *Faerie Queene,* the desire for fame, the delight in romance and adventure, pride in the glory of England, and concern for moral and religious edification are combined in a comprehensive design.

Nothing in this broad concept of the heroic poem ruled out the possibility of using Biblical material as subject matter, nor were there many expressions of doubt about the propriety of a Biblical epic. Although the suitability of Scriptural material had been questioned by some Italian and French critics,[7] both Tasso and Du Bartas had argued strongly for specifically Biblical as well as general Christian materials. The Continental arguments over the propriety of Christian machines and marvels as against those of the pagan classics apparently stirred little interest in England. Not until the second half of the century did English critics, influenced primarily by French neoclassical theories, seriously debate the advantages or disadvantages of Biblical materials.

Although English neoclassical criticism had very little to do with the works under consideration here, a brief outline of the elements of this criticism which concern the problem of using Biblical materials can suggest some of the difficulties faced by the earlier poets. In 1650 two English treatises by Davenant and Hobbes foreshadowed the neoclassical theory of the epic. In the preface to *Gondibert,* Davenant argued for a Christian subject, but took issue with Tasso for using Christian machinery in fantastic episodes.[8] His argument rested upon his belief that the Bible was essentially a body of divine and historical truth and that the Christian report of the supernatural world was fact, not fable. Moral truths could better be portrayed poetically by the judicious invention of an appropriate non-Biblical fable than by the indecorous use of divine history. Although he made no specific comments on Biblical heroic narratives, he did speak with profound contempt of the mass of devotional works which were being produced by incompetent writers inspired only by their consciences: "and the newest of such great volumes, being usually but transcriptions or translations, differ so much from the Ancients as later daies from those of old, which difference is no more than an alteration of names by removing the *Ethnicks*[9] to make way for the Saints."[10] He would seem to imply here that the slavish imitation of classical form for a Christian subject might lead to something inappropriate or ridiculous.

Hobbes's letter in reply to Davenant's preface showed him to be in general agreement with these opinions. He was even more strongly opposed to any use of the supernatural or marvelous in purely human affairs that strained the limits of probability.[11] Davenant and Hobbes thus stood at mid-century in partial opposition to some of the conventional practices and concepts of the Christian epic. Both regarded the Bible as history of so distinct and precise a kind that it could not readily be used as material for invented action without violating the principle of decorum. Furthermore, they rejected the notion that because many pagan myths seemed to have parallels in Old Testament history, the pagan and the Biblical could be treated in the same manner or, worse, mixed together in fabulous episodes. If they were irritated by the efforts of the religious poets to achieve the effects of heroic poetry, however, they were in full concurrence with the movement which found in the Christian emphasis upon the cosmic and celestial action the proper material for the epic. Hobbes made the heroic almost synonymous with the sublime: "For there is in Princes, and men of conspicuous power (anciently call'd *Heroes*) a lustre and influence upon the rest of men, resembling that of the Heavens...."[12]

Although Cowley had close associations with Davenant and Hobbes, he was much more confident and enthusiastic about both the possibilities and the propriety of using Biblical materials for an epic. In his view there was no worthier matter to be found than that of divine history as recorded in the Word of God: "...why will not the actions of Sampson afford as plentiful matter as the Labors of Hercules? why is not Jeptha's Daughter as good a woman as Iphigenia? and the friendship of David and Jonathan more worthy celebration than that of Theseus and Perithous?...All the Books of the Bible are either already most admirable, and exalted pieces of Poesie, or are the best Materials in the world for it."[13] Cowley believed that strict imitation of classical epic form, particularly of Virgil's *Aeneid,* was the best way to success—"the examples of Homer and Virgil...we should do ill to forsake to imitate others."[14] As a young man in his twenties, he had been enthusiastic about Du Bartas's *Divine Weekes* and was familiar with some of the French and English attempts to cast Biblical narratives in classical form. In 1656, however, he had grown impatient with those efforts, which fell short of his own ambitious design for the *Davideis,* and remarked in the preface, "...For if any man design to compose a Sacred Poem, by only turning a story of the Scripture, like Mr. Quarles, or some other godly matter, like Mr.

Heywood of Angels, into Rhyme, He is so far from elevating Poesie that he only abases Divinity."[15] Cowley, though probably influenced in his choice of a Biblical subject matter by the precedent of Du Bartas and by the enthusiasm of such contemporaries as Quarles, determined to adhere strictly to the model of Virgil rather than the Renaissance models of Tasso, Du Bartas, or Spenser.

Milton left no fully worked out statement of epic theory. Of considerable interest, however, are his relatively early musings in *The Reason of Church Government* (1641) about the epic poem he planned to write.

> Time serves not now, and perhaps I might seem too profuse to give any certain account of what the mind at home in the spacious circuits of her musings hath liberty to propose to her self, ... whether that Epick form whereof the two poems of Homer, and those other two of Virgil and Tasso are a diffuse, and the book of Job a brief model: or whether the rules of Aristotle herein are strictly to be kept, or nature to be follow'd, which in them that know art, and use judgement is no transgression, but an inriching of art.[16]

Unlike Cowley, however, Milton had considered a patriotic heroic poem, an Arthuriad in the Renaissance manner, and for this the *Faerie Queene* was the great English precedent. But Spenser's epic was not only a patriotic poem; it also provided in the first two books the theme of the pilgrimage of the soul, and the allegorical portrayal of the warfare between good and evil. Milton was attracted also to the hexameral materials and the story of the Fall made popular by Du Bartas's epic of Creation with its theme of universal history. When Milton's plans for a patriotic subject were changed by the course of events in England, he turned back to these traditional Christian themes rather than, like Cowley, to the neoclassical concept of a Virgilian form strictly imposed upon an Old Testament figure possessing some of the classical heroic characteristics. Milton's predilection for these great themes is certainly suggested in the passage from *The Reason of Church Government*, though in a Pindaric rather than Homeric vein: "... to celebrate in glorious and lofty Hymnes the throne and equipage of Gods Almightinesse, and what he works, and what he suffers to be wrought with high providence in his Church, to sing the victorious agonies of Martyrs and Saints...."[17]

If Cowley and Milton at mid-century reflect only indirectly the influence of neoclassical theories of the epic as they were developing on the Continent, it is not surprising that English critical writings in the first half of the century reveal little interest in the concept of the sacred heroic poem. Jonson, the most classical of the critics, wrote very briefly in his *Discoveries* of the epic in general, and favorably only of a patriotic poem based on King Arthur as a Christian hero. It is impossible to conceive, however, that the English poets were wholly unaware of the French experiments with the Biblical epic in the sixteenth and seventeenth centuries. In a recent study of the French works, Professor R. A. Sayce[18] distinguishes two main groups of such poems: the first in the period to 1620, containing the works of the Pléiade group, Du Bartas, and Montchrestien; the second group beginning with Saint-Amant's *Moyse Sauvé* (1653) and continuing to the end of the century. He characterizes the first group as following the Bible with both a concern for literal accuracy and an enthusiasm for great literary possibilities which produced a certain freedom in combining Biblical and pagan elements. The second group he characterizes as having a greater concern for conventional morality and for what were considered to be the proper rules and style of the epic, a concern which led to a deformation of the simple grandeur of the Scriptural texts.[19]

A comparative study of the French and English Biblical works of this period, particularly at the beginning of the century, perhaps needs to be undertaken, but the parallels are numerous enough to warrant a tentative conclusion that some of the English poets were influenced by French models. The influence of Du Bartas has been thoroughly explored, but it is likely that such early works as Du Bellay's *La Monomachie de David et Goliat* (1560) and Pierre de Brach's poem with the same title (1560), both epic fragments or episodes, were models for Drayton's short poem, *David and Golia,* written at the beginning of the century, though not printed until 1630. One difference is apparent, however. Where the earlier French poets used pagan gods and machinery with considerable freedom—De Brach, for example, bringing in Jupiter and Mars as lords of thunder and war—the earlier English poets such as Sabie and Drayton adhered much more closely to the text of the Bible, and embellished or expanded their descriptions without resort to pagan machinery. The later English poets such as Aylett and Cowley, however, reflect the influence of the French and Italian models and theories. Certain conventions—the identifying of pagan deities and furies with angels and demons, and the use of tapestries, dream visions, or angelic messengers to introduce epic digressions—have their counterparts in earlier Italian or French works.

Such, then, were some of the theories, the models, and the conventions that were available for English poets aspiring to write the ideal Christian epic based on Scriptural truth. It is evident that as guides, these were of varied and limited usefulness, and provided no easy path to the realization of the ideal. At the beginning of the century, the problem of adjusting Biblical materials to heroic form based on that of classical models was certainly the principal one, and the various solutions of this problem will be examined in the following chapters.

Related to this problem was the question of the nature of the instruction which a Biblical heroic poem should offer. For the religious poet, it was not the humanist or patriotic interest in the virtue of the ruler and the health of the body politic which dominated his sense of purpose, but rather his concern with the spiritual health of the individual soul. His purpose was thus in a sense devotional, but devotional poetry was primarily an expression of the subjective and personal interests of the poet. Narrative poetry, particularly heroic narrative, was essentially objective, and did not easily lend itself to devotional commentary. If the poet adhered to the widely accepted principle that the epic should follow the model set by Homer and Virgil, then he was committed to an extended narration in verse of illustrious action. The problem lay not so much in his use of Biblical figures in place of the pagan gods and heroes as it did in the fact that the Biblical materials immediately introduced religious associations which were not always in harmony with the epic action. The sin of David with Bathsheba and the wrath of Achilles could be compared as illustrations of the hero's limitations and wrongful acts, but the religious significance of David in many other respects made further comparison with Achilles difficult. The temptation for the Biblical poet would be to develop the religious significance at the expense of the epic action. Du Bartas had provided one example of a fairly strict classical heroic narrative in his *Judith,* but his greatest influence stemmed from the *Divine Weekes,* in which devotional commentary often submerged the epic design. Before Cowley and Milton, the English Biblical poets had made no clear separation between their devotional and narrative interests. Quarles did try to keep his narration distinct in his Biblical "Histories," but nevertheless felt impelled to add long passages of devotional meditation and commentary to each of the narrative sections.

Not all the religious poets, furthermore, were prepared to limit their didactic or devotional interests for the sake of rivaling secular or classical achievements. The traditional Christian medieval forms continued to satisfy the popular demand for explicit piety and conventional morality. As a result, during the first decades of the century, in such works as Giles Fletcher's *Christ's Victorie,* medieval and classical forms were often mixed in more or less arbitrary ways. There was always the danger for the poet of assuming that mere statement of piety carried over to the reader the same feeling which inspired it. Part of the problem, therefore, was to avoid relying too much upon conventional phraseology, yet at the same time to avoid taking too great a liberty with the Biblical text.

The medieval tradition of allegorical interpretation was another conventional element which was to continue its hold on the imagination of the religious poet. Although for Protestants the Bible was the chief authority in matters of doctrine and practice, the long tradition of exegesis and commentary remained important as a necessary adjunct to Biblical interpretation. The reformers had attempted to counter the traditional fourfold scholastic interpretation of Scripture by placing greater emphasis upon the literal sufficiency of the Word of God, but they could not root out the long-established habit of reading the Bible for secondary meanings. Similarly, the practice of allegorizing the fable and machinery of classical epics in the light of Christian truths remained no less habitual in Renaissance thought. Although the narrative poets might reject allegory as a mode of expression for the literal and historical truths of the Bible, they could not ignore the secondary meanings and applications made traditional by the commentaries.

The extent to which the hexameral commentaries of David Pareus, Benedict Pererius, Marin Mersenne, and Cornelius de Lapide were used by Protestant poets of the seventeenth century has been well established.[20] The traditional exegesis of other parts of the Bible, particularly that of the early Fathers, Jerome, Gregory, and Augustine, were equally well known in Catholic works and in such Protestant forms as Calvin's *Institutes.*[21] The commentary tradition was especially important, as

we shall see, because it maintained in an increasingly rational-
istic age the unified Christian story of universal history and of
the cosmic drama. It was not only the hexameral tradition which
helped to determine the pattern of the seventeenth-century Biblical epic, but also the whole exegetical tradition as it affected
the concept of such figures as Samson,[22] and even the concept
of Christ.[23]

The development of Biblical narrative poetry toward greater
imitation of classical heroic form thus required a number of
adjustments which would allow for the poet's devotional and
didactic aims and which would enable the poet to develop his
themes within the framework of the Christian rather than the
classical design. At the beginning of the century, Du Bartas
and Spenser provided the only models available for a specifically
Protestant epic. Neither was essentially classical in form, although both were epic in magnitude and used many features
of the classical epic. The *Divine Weekes* served as a model which
showed one way of combining Biblical themes and didactic
interests on a vast scale. The *Faerie Queene* supplied the model
of how to portray in heroic manner such traditional Christian
themes as the pilgrimage of the soul. Although Du Bartas and
Spenser gave impetus to the seventeenth-century interest in
heroic narrative poetry, their epics did not solve the problems
peculiar to the writing of a Biblical epic. It is in the works of
the minor narrative poets between Spenser and Milton that the
search for the needed unity of action and the properly Christian heroic protagonist can be most clearly seen and demonstrated.

Most of these minor works belong to that category usually
relegated to the passing reference or the learned footnote. The
usual method of classifying them has been to relate them to
some dominant influence. A great many have been typed as
they reflected the influence of Spenser and Du Bartas, or were

medieval remnants, Renaissance fashions, or classical imitations. Such a method has been inadequate to describe the more precise characteristics of the works. Thus far, only Lily B. Campbell's very broad description of the "cult" of the Christian Muse[24] has established a limited set of characteristics common to most of these works. A different kind of classification, one that takes into account the various subjects and forms, is necessary. Such a classification of the works will be found in the Appendix of this study. A brief comment here upon this classification will suffice to indicate the kinds of experimentation in the first half of the century, and to suggest some of the attempted combinations and adjustments of subject and form.

There are three general forms into which the Biblical narrative poetry can be grouped: *discursive, allegorical,* and *classical heroic.* These forms are by no means always pure and distinct, but they can be distinguished according to their relative dominance in the various works and as they reflect the particular interest and approach of the poets. The term "discursive" is intended to suggest both the element of discourse, either formal or personal, and the use of digressions to allow the poet to indulge his concern for devotion or didacticism. Du Bartas provided the chief model for this kind of treatment; his materials were primarily those devotional or learned commonplaces made popular by medieval and Renaissance commentaries and encyclopedic compendia of Christian knowledge. The term "allegorical" is used to mean the figurative narrative form best exemplified by Spenser's *Faerie Queene.* Allegorical storytelling had a long history, but its use was clearly sanctioned by the parables of Christ, and such Old Testament parables as that of the prophet Nathan concerning David's adultery. For the Protestant poet, however, the literal meaning of the Biblical text was regarded as sufficient for teaching, and required no secondary form of presentation. The allegorical form, nevertheless, continued to be both popular and useful in treating non-Biblical Christian themes such as the pilgrimage of the soul and the warfare between good and evil for the soul, which were combined in the ardently Puritan dream allegory of Bunyan's *Pilgrim's Progress*.

The classical heroic category, as the name suggests, includes Scriptural narratives which were in part or in whole attempts to imitate the form of classical heroic poetry. Some of the epic features—invocations to the muse, grand diction, epic similes, and adornments by the use of the marvelous—were widely imitated even if they had no real relationship to the theme or structure. The most important feature for the classification, however, was the direct narrative form which told the story without recourse to elaborate allegory or discursive morality.

In the chapters to follow, the Biblical poems will be examined in terms of the relationship of the discursive, classical heroic, and allegorical forms, and the three principal subject matters, hexameral, Old Testament, and New Testament. All three subject matters were potentially, and actually in many poems, bound together within the all-encompassing view of the working out of Divine Providence in universal history. The classification is useful primarily because it reveals how some of the earlier experiments within the limited areas proved that the full-scale Christian epic could not be restricted to any one segment of the historical process. Although most of the hexameral materials were derived from extra-Biblical sources, these materials contributed strongly to the concept of God's plan evolving from Creation through the course of history to the Last Judgment. The Old Testament materials contributed specific examples of heroic action that could be viewed typologically as "Christian." The New Testament subjects, though limited by the difficulties of treating the figure of Christ directly, placed the emphasis upon the significance of the central event in universal history and upon the supreme heroic action that made possible, despite human limitations, heroism for the individual Christian.

The most noteworthy fact is the almost complete correlation between the categories of form and subject matter: the hexameral subjects are nearly always treated in a discursive form, New Testament subjects in an allegorical form, and Old Testament subjects in a classical heroic form. This correlation supports the conclusion that the interest in both hexameral and New Testament subjects remained primarily devotional and traditional in nature. The form of the narrative, either discursive or allegorical, was adopted to facilitate the treatment of material which was not readily presentable in objective forms. The correlation between the Old Testament subjects and the classical heroic form supports the conclusion that the search for the ideal Biblical epic led the narrative poets to look first for examples of human heroism in Old Testament history, examples that could compare with the classical pagan heroes, rather than resort to allegorical or fictionalized action.

Although the Old Testament would seem, at first glance, to provide a number of illustrious figures comparable to those of Homer or Virgil in both positive and negative attributes, these "Christian" figures could not in practice so readily be substituted for the pagan. In order to understand the difficulties involved, we need to trace the way in which these figures had first to evolve from medieval moral examples into personages whose histories were individually of human interest, capable of being developed on a heroic scale. At the beginning of the century, the poets who were interested in the Old Testament figures as historically true and very human representatives of "Christian" heroism could validly claim that they were meeting the requirements of such broad Elizabethan definitions of the heroic poem as Puttenham's "Historical examples of valor and virtue."[25] These figures could be regarded as legitimate subjects if they were worthy or illustrious examples. Very few of the Old Testament personages, however, were worthy in all respects. Some, of course, could be compared with a classical hero like Achilles in that they possessed major weaknesses of character which helped to produce epic conflicts and vicissitudes. Indeed, many of them were essentially negative examples, and had been traditionally treated as such in the compendia of moral *exempla* presenting the fall of illustrious men. In Chaucer's *Monk's Tale* and Lydgate's *Fall of Princes,* Biblical personages were presented together with classical figures of myth or history, and with persons and events of more recent times. The *Monk's Tale* appropriately began with the fall of Lucifer and went on with the fall of Adam, then of Samson, to be followed by the story of Samson's pagan counterpart, Hercules. Before he was cut off, the Monk had ranged forward to the tragedies of Nebuchadnezzar, Belshazzar, and Holofernes.

The continued popularity of these tragic stories and compilations of moral examples in the sixteenth century led to the ambitious undertaking, prompted by humanist and patriotic interest, of the *Mirror for Magistrates*. Although this work continued the medieval tradition of the moral illustration, the didacticism shifted from purely theological to political and humanistic spheres. Its influence, however, led Anthony Munday to imitate the form in his *Mirrour of Mutabilitie* (1579), in which he turned almost wholly to the Bible for his examples. His personages were all clearly linked with various vices, beginning in the first part with the Seven Deadly Sins: Pride illustrated by Nebuchadnezzar, Envy by Herod, Lechery by David, Avarice by Judas, and so forth. In the second part, he illustrated both vices and virtues as they were found in one person: Solomon represented not only inordinate love of women but also the virtue of Sapience; Samson illustrated both the vice of yielding to the weaker sex and the virtue of Magnanimity.

The Mirror literature thus helped to establish a liking for historical narrative and for a didactic form which portrayed rather than propounded its moral. The traditional medieval compendia of *exempla* had been conceived as instruments of rhetoric, useful in sermon or exhortation to "prove" the need for faith or sound morality. The fortunes or misfortunes of great men were particularly effective, for they could yield examples of both vices and virtues on an imposing scale. Narrative poetry of the Mirror or Complaint type helped to further the transition from the medieval rhetorical use of undifferentiated moral examples to the Renaissance exploration of the individual and dramatic aspects of the worthy example from history. The fall of illustrious men provided rich material for tragedy, but the noble and virtuous acts as well as the wrong or "wrathful" acts of great men were also fit subjects for heroic poetry.

The transition to the view of Scriptural personages as potential subjects for heroic poetry was a slow one; and, it must be concluded, very few survived the transition to become clearly heroic. Many of them, such as Ahab or Jezebel, were so obviously illustrations of evil that their histories could never supply the grandeur or nobility of action felt necessary for the epic. Joseph, David, Susanna, Judith, Job, and Esther were the figures which attracted the poets most often, but they represented kinds of heroism that were not easily paralleled in the classical models. The transition involved a very necessary shift in the view of what constituted the heroic act and what qualities the Christian hero should possess. For the religious poet, Christian virtues transcended those of the pagan, and the term "worthy" came to be interpreted in a specifically Christian sense to mean heroism in the struggle with all manifestations of evil, both in the world and in the spirit.

Such a concept of heroism did not develop at once, nor did the Elizabethan concept of the heroic poem really point in this direction. Sixteenth-century Biblical narratives and paraphrases were, for the most part, transitional works of indistinct form, but they did help to make possible a shift away from older forms of didacticism involving allegory or rhetorical morality, and furthered the interest in the objective narrative form. By the end of the century a few poets such as Francis Sabie were beginning to adopt classical heroic features in combination with the traditional elements. The opening lines of Sabie's *The Olde Worlde's Tragedie* (1596), the story of Noah and the Flood, sounded the epic note:

> I sing of horrors sad and dreadful rage,
> Of stratagems wrought in the former age,
> Contagious vice, and in conclusion,
> Of massacres, death, and confusion.[26]

But what followed immediately was hardly heroic—a lengthy procession of the vices in the medieval manner.

Sabie's *David and Bethsabe* (1596) provides a much clearer illustration of the way in which the Old Testament figure was evolving into a subject of historical and potentially heroic narrative. Sabie treated David primarily as a moral example, but drew attention to the nature of David's struggle with temptation and his heavy remorse after he had fallen. The whole incident is given significance in terms of God's relationship to the individual human being:

> O rouse not up from sleep thy kingly head;
> Least by mischaunce thou fall into a trap,
> See heere of mans fragilitie a map:
> Thou canst not (*David*) needs must thou upstart,
> Thy God will haue thee know how frayle thou art.[27]

Sabie's choice of David, not as the heroic figure who slew Goliath, but as an example of temptation, fall, and repentance, is indicative of the direction in which the concept of Christian heroism was to move.

The theme of temptation or moral choice as a test of the hero's virtue was to become of primary importance, but, as examples from history often showed, the hero was not always able to make the proper choice, and fell into sin. The suffering which followed, however, could be viewed as a test of the hero's fortitude and spiritual strength. In the Christian view, there was not only the heroism of the active struggle with evil forces, but also the heroism of sacrifice and submission to the Will of God in order that greater good might be achieved, the *victorious* suffering of the martyrs and saints. Furthermore, the contest with evil was seen not only as a test of the Christian hero's nobility and spiritual strength, but also as the means whereby he might gain greater wisdom and faith. Trial and suffering began to emerge as the chief measures of the Christian hero, whose virtue and steadfastness were thus exemplified and proved. These qualities correspond closely to the heroic formula of wisdom and courage (*sapientia et fortitudo*), which E. R. Curtius has traced as the principal theme of heroism from antiquity to the Renaissance.[28] The strength of body and mind glorified in classical times became, in the Christian view, courage and steadfastness in the active life of the world, and spiritual wisdom and faith in the contemplative life. The Christian emphasis tended to fall upon the perfection of the contemplative life, that is, upon the growth of spiritual wisdom and faith. Yet a passive virtue was incomplete and unfulfilled unless it was manifested in the active life, which in turn provided the experience necessary for further growth. The Renaissance ideal was to find a balance between or a combination of the active and the contemplative virtues in a single hero.[29] This ideal combination Spenser sought to exemplify by allegorical means in the *Faerie Queene,* especially in the figures of the Red Cross Knight and Sir Guyon. The periods of instruction and preparation for further trial which both underwent showed the necessity for a balance between active courage and spiritual strength. In Spenser's epic the Biblical poets had fully worked out examples of heroes who illustrated the testing of Christian virtues and the attainment of greater spiritual knowledge through the experience of suffering and repentance.

The Old Testament figures, even though they were historically true examples, could not have been made subjects of heroic poetry if their actions and motives seemed remote and alien to the Christian reader. Old Testament history, if viewed only as the chronicle of the affairs of the ancient Hebrew people, would have lacked immediate appeal for the sixteenth- or seventeenth-century Christian. Old Testament history, however, had been made an essential part of a larger context in traditional interpretation. Not only had the Old Testament been read in the light of the New, but many of the Hebrew heroes and prophets had been interpreted typologically as figures of Christ. As Erich Auerbach has pointed out, contrasting the Hebraic and the Greek sense of history:

The claim of the Old Testament stories to represent universal history, their insistent relation—a relation constantly redefined by conflicts—to a single and hidden God, who yet shows himself and who guides universal history by promise and exaction, gives these stories an entirely different perspective from any the Homeric poems can possess. As a composition, the Old Testament is incomparably less unified than the Homeric poems; it is more obviously pieced together—but the various components all belong to one concept of universal history and its interpretation.[30]

Auerbach suggests a new term, "figural," for the interpretation employed in this universal context. Adam, Noah, and Samson can be regarded as "figures," not symbols, of Christ; as such they are incomplete, for in themselves they fall far short of the ideal. They stand for the limited human potential for good which was eventually to be realized or fulfilled in Christ's Incarnation and Passion. In the span of time between Creation and the Last Judgment, Christ is the climax of the Divine Plan of action; in the interval before Christ, there are the figures foreshadowing Christ; and afterward come the imitators of Christ, the saints and martyrs. That these figural elements were often inseparable from the original Biblical materials in everyday thinking can be seen in the conventional seventeenth-century view of such figures as Noah and Samson.[31] The important fact is that the literal reality of the Old Testament stories was never lost sight of, the concrete never submerged in the abstract.

The figure of Job was particularly significant, for Job was closely bound, as the chief example, with the theological concept of Christian patience and forbearance in trial or suffering. Job's nobility and steadfastness, together with his eventual restoration, was well suited to "heroic" treatment, as in Sylvester's *Job Triumphant* and Quarles's *Job Militant*. As a figure of Christ, Job was significant also because his story posed the problem of justifying God's ways to man to explain the heroic virtue of Christian fortitude in the midst of inscrutable and terrifying events. It is little wonder that Milton saw the Book of Job as his best model for a brief epic. To justify God's ways toward Job required a new concept of heroism, combining classical nobility and Christian humility but more universal in appeal than the rather specialized heroism of the saints and martyrs. The Book of Job was in many ways the most important link between the concepts and figures of the Old Testament and the fulfillment and realization of their "historical" potential in the New Testament.

The apocalyptic view of world history reinforced the Christian, especially Puritan, interpretations of the workings of Providence.[32] Revelation and the Book of Daniel were widely read as prophetic of the course of human degeneration before the promised Second Coming. The general theme that things will get worse before they get better in a historical process could apply in a mystical sense to the fortunes of the individual soul. In his battle with Satan, the Christian hero could expect to experience the worst torments of spiritual despair and pessimism before his faith and his fortitude in trial justified his hope of salvation. The pattern of temptation, fall, suffering, and repentance as seen in this vast perspective became the archetypal pattern for both the individual and mankind as a whole.

The Biblical narrative poets thus came to concentrate upon temptation, trial, and suffering as the most significant experiences for the Christian hero and the chief measures of his faith, virtue, and fortitude. In this respect, they remained within the bounds of the Renaissance concept of heroic poetry, yet they were led to put a somewhat different emphasis upon the nature and setting of Christian heroic action. If they dealt with the historical reality of Biblical stories and personages, they were able to adopt in some measure the objective manner of classical narrative poetry, but their interest still lay in the "inner conflict" of the heroic example. If they were resolute in avoiding allegory or devotional comment, the problem was to portray the true nature of the Christian struggle with evil. The answer lay in the traditional Christian view of the world and of universal history. The nature of the heroic action was made clear when represented in relation to the cosmic setting of the great struggle between good and evil. It is in this sense that Milton was prepared to "sing the victorious agonies of Martyrs and Saints." The Biblical materials could illustrate not only types of Christian heroism but also the vast design of Providence in human history. Certainly by the time Milton began to work out his design for *Paradise Lost* the elements necessary for this concept of heroism were all present. Perhaps the vitality and thoroughness of Milton's and Bunyan's expressions of the concept can best be judged when their works are measured against Richard Steele's statement of the concept in "The Christian Hero" at the beginning of the next century. The solid core of faith and fortitude found in Milton's and Bunyan's concept of heroism was already beginning to soften into sentiment and abstractions:

But to capacitate ones self for this hard Work, how necessary is that Sublime and Heroick Virtue, Meekness, a Virtue which seems the very Characteristick of a Christian, and arises from a great, not a groveling Idea of things: For as certainly as Pride proceeds from a mean and narrow view of the little advantages about a Man's self, so Meekness is founded on the extended Contemplation of the Place we bear in the Universe.[33]

Perhaps the seventeenth-century Biblical epic poets would understand the term "meekness" in reference to the idea of submission to Divine Providence, but it is doubtful that they would have seen meekness as the virtue most "Characteristick of a Christian." The general concept of the exemplary hero had been given a special Christian meaning by emphasis on the need for an active testing of faith through trial and suffering, which would lead to growth in spiritual understanding. For the Puritans in particular, stirred by the eloquence of their preachers, it was, in the words of William Haller, "the dramatic images of temptation, struggle, and triumph which the newly popularized Bible put into their hands."[34]

The seven deadly sins are once more whistled up, but from being dialectical abstractions they have become furies leaping upon the heart of the sinner as upon a stage. The scene enacted upon that stage is henceforth to be the focus of all attention. It is to be the drama of sin and grace, of the war between Christ and Satan, experienced immediately in the soul.... The men and women ... are asked to see themselves as Adam and Eve hearkening to the serpent in the garden. And we as we listen with them to the preacher's eloquence may catch a forward glimpse of the Puritan legend of the wayfaring, warfaring Christian, of the Puritan epic of the fall and redemption of man.[35]

In the chapters to follow, we shall analyze the themes and structure of representative works which exemplify the three types of Biblical material. Each type—hexameral, Old Testament, or New Testament—posed problems of treatment that had to be solved before a successful Biblical epic could be written. In the last analysis, no one of the three subjects could succeed independently, for it was in the nature of the Christian world picture that the significance of the cosmic and the individual human actions were inextricably bound together within the scope of the universal drama. The narrative poets before Milton tried with varying degrees of success to find in a heroic form the best way of relating the experiences of the individual Christian to the archetypal patterns implicit in God's mysterious but merciful design for man as set forth in the Bible. None, before Milton, succeeded in achieving the unity and coherence required of the fully realized epic. In this sense, Milton was perhaps justified in his claim that he was pursuing "Things unattempted yet in Prose or Rhyme."

CHAPTER II

THE HEXAMERAL TRADITION

THE TERM "hexameral" is now used to designate not only the works dealing with Creation, but also those which deal with any of the subjects that had become associated with the hexameral tradition. In one sense, this tradition was not Biblical, but a development of the exegetical commentaries on Genesis. It was, nevertheless, in the sixteenth and seventeenth centuries so strongly established in the stream of literary tradition that in normal thinking it was inseparable from the Book of Genesis. The *Hexaemeron* of Basil, Bishop of Caesarea, A.D. 370–379, was the earliest Christian work dealing exclusively with Creation, and from this work until the Renaissance the body of hexameral writings increased in volume and scope. Medieval writers often appended discussions of the attributes of God, of the angels, the fall of the rebellious angels, and the fall of Adam and Eve, and this led to consideration of the nature of the Incarnation and the Redemption, and eventually to the Last Judgment.

The basic theme remained the six days of Creation; but two other themes, the revolt and fall of Satan and his followers and the temptation and fall of man, developed strong interest of their own in association with the basic theme. The union of the three themes in literary form became a kind of trilogy which Thibaut termed "the celestial cycle." With this "cycle" was associated other material from Genesis such as the subsequent history of man down to Noah and the Flood, all of which had received extensive treatment in the commentaries, and was traditionally included in "histories" of the world. Sir Walter Raleigh, significantly used the word "memorable" in the caption, "Memorable things between the Fall of Adam and the

[33]

Flood of Noah."[1] As Professor Grant McColley has concluded: "During the Sixteenth and Seventeenth Centuries, by far the most popular book for commentary, for literary paraphrase, and for incidental use was Genesis. So vast was the learning expended upon this book, that the last of the great commentaries, the *Questions on Genesis* of Marin Mersenne, required more than fifteen hundred large folio columns to reach discussion of Tubal and Jubal Cain."[2]

Professor McColley goes even farther to suggest that paraphrases of Biblical history subsequent to Genesis were part of the hexameral tradition, citing the Caedmonian *Genesis* and Milton's *Paradise Lost* as examples.[3] Such paraphrases, of course, were summaries of the significant events of Old Testament history leading up to Christ, and were meant to be viewed and interpreted in the light of the New Testament and the Christian concept of world history. The elaboration of this view of universal history by Augustine in the *City of God,* particularly Books XI to XVII, covering Biblical history from the Creation to the last of the prophets before Christ, is but one of the many treatments of hexameral materials which were well known to the seventeenth-century poets. According to the most recent editors of Du Bartas, there were over a hundred twenty-five hexamera, sermons, treatises, and poems from Philo Judaeus (ca. A.D. 40) down to 1578.[4] Many of these would have been unknown or forgotten in the Renaissance, but they are significant primarily because they show the continuity of a tradition which was still so vital in the early seventeenth century that Raleigh devoted all of Book I and twenty-three chapters of Book II of his *History of the World* (1614) to Biblical events from Creation to the last prophets. Independent paraphrases of Scriptural stories about historical personages from Joseph onward should, however, be distinguished from the hexameral paraphrases,

---

[1] For notes to chapter ii see page 144.

since they were expansions and elaborations rather than summaries, and were to some extent isolated temporarily from the
basic context of world history.

The immense interest in the hexameral materials helped to
reinforce the practice of figural interpretation with its Creation-
to-Doomsday frame of reference and its emphasis upon Christ
as the climax of the universal action. This cosmic frame of
reference provided the religious poets of the sixteenth and
seventeenth centuries with a coherent pattern within which
human experience gained meaning in relation to a divine reality.
It not only furnished the key to orthodox interpretation of the
Bible but also satisfied men's curiosity regarding the nature of
the world, both in substance and spirit. The hexameral tradition, then, supplied the principal materials for understanding
the world, the mystery of its Creation, the state of man through
the course of history, and the ultimate purpose and end, according to God's plan.

Du Bartas's *Divine Weekes* stands as the prototype of the
Renaissance hexameral epic. The work is so well known as a
result of recent scholarship on the Renaissance and on Milton
that it is hardly necessary to describe it in detail. In the following analysis, the work will be considered primarily as it contributed to the development of the Christian epic design in the
first half of the seventeenth century, and as it represented for
the English narrative poets a possible model for the combining
of Biblical materials and heroic form.

Although the conjunction of hexameral materials and epic
treatment seemed perfectly natural in a didactic poem at the
beginning of the century, the instructive rather than the epic
features were the real measure of value or success in such poems
as the *Divine Weekes,* and many were prepared to forgive any
structural weakness in a work if they were edified by the truth
and wisdom to be found in it. Thomas Lodge provided a typical

observation on the *Divine Weekes* from this point of view:

> I protest that *Bartas* is as much delightfull as any Greeke, Latine, or French Author that we can light upon, who ever hath bestowed his stile and study to speake of God and his Workes. Moreover, I avow him in the first ranke of Writers, either ancient or Moderne, that ever intermixed profit with pleasure ... I consider alwayes the honorable profit I may draw from him ... in a short space we shall beare away the treasures of divine and humane Science.[5]

Even in Du Bartas's own day, however, there were serious criticisms of his work as an epic and accusations that he violated the rules of Aristotle and of other classical authorities and models. So extensive were his didactic digressions that unity was sacrificed, but his immense popularity rested upon just this discursive mingling of profit and pleasure. Du Bartas met criticism, nevertheless, by explaining that it had not been his intention to write a purely epic poem in the classical manner. His reply was set forth in the *Brief Advertissement sur sa première et seconde Sepmaine* (1584), given here in the translation of Thomas Lodge:

> Others ... accuse me either that I was ignorant, or that I have neglected the Rules which Aristotle and Horace prescribe as proper to heroicke Poets. If I persisted in my Negative, it may be they should be very much puzzled to prove their intention: but to put them out of all doubt, let them learne of me, that my second Weeke is not (no more then my first) a worke purely Epique or Heroique, but in part Panegyricall, in part Propheticall, and in part Didascatique. Heere I simply set downe the History, there I move affections: Heere I call upon God, there I yeeld him thankes: heere I sing a Hymne unto him & there I vomit out a Satyre against the Vices of mine Age: Heere I instruct men in good manners, there in pietie: Heere I discourse of naturall things, and other-where I praise good spirits.[6]

It is ironic that Du Bartas had to defend himself also against attacks from the other side, criticizing his use of pagan classical imagery and references. In his reply, he argued that it was traditional to use such references but that he hoped they would eventually disappear altogether: "And when I use them [Pagan divinities] it is with *metonymie* or while making some allusions to their fables, a practice which has been followed till now by those who have made Christian poems. Poetry has been for so long in the possession of these fabulous names that it is impossible to dispossess them save step by step."[7]

An outline of the structure of the *Divine Weekes* will suffice to point out the features of particular interest to this study. A distinction should be made between the *First Weeke* and the *Second Weeke,* because Du Bartas's plan for the second undertaking was much more ambitious than for the first. His plan in the *First Weeke* was simply to recount the wonders and mysteries of the Creation from the nature of Chaos on the first day to the divinely appointed Sabbath on the seventh. Along the way he undertook to present the best of the commentary answers to such questions as when the angels were created, what Time and Space were, and whether God had any attributes. The second day was devoted to the Elements, the third to the Sea and Earth, the fourth to the Heavens, Sun, and Moon, the fifth to the Fishes and Fowls, and the sixth to the Beasts and Man. The fact that the *First Weeke* runs to over six thousand lines indicates the degree to which Du Bartas amplified with encyclopedic, commentary, and devotional material the bare account in the first two chapters of Genesis.

In the *Second Weeke,* Du Bartas planned to treat the whole of Biblical history contained in the Old and New Testaments and to complete the portrayal of the vast design of universal history by devoting the last section to Doomsday and the Eternal Sabbath. It is noteworthy that in the *Brief Advertissement* (1584) Du Bartas pointed out Augustine's *City of God* as one of the most important sources for his plan in the *Second Weeke*:

"je les renvoie au dernier chapitre de la *Cité de Dieu* de S. Augustin, duquel j'ay pris et le titre, et l'argument, et la division de ce livre."[8] The historical nature of his materials required him to construct a new design within the framework of the original seven-day pattern and forced him to exercise a greater degree of selection. Each day was to be devoted to figures of major importance: (1) Adam, (2) Noah, (3) Abraham, (4) David, (5) Zedechiah, (6) Messias, (7) The Eternal Sabbath. Du Bartas further divided each of the completed four days into four parts, an elaboration unnecessary in the first week.

The first day, centered upon Adam and running to nearly three thousand lines in Sylvester's translation, may be taken as an example. Under the subtitle, *Eden,* Du Bartas gave a long description of the Garden before the Fall and made an extended comparison with the city of Paris, which Sylvester saw fit to change to his own beloved London. In the next section, "The Imposture," the machinations of "Hell's prince" in the guise of the serpent lead to the temptation and fall of Eve and subsequently of Adam. Sylvester was no plodding translator, but frequently exercised his own fancy, as in this explanation of why Satan should have taken the guise of a serpent:

> But this stands sure, how-ever else it went,
> Th' old Serpent serv'd as Satan's instrument
> To charme in *Eden,* with a strong illusion,
> Our silly Grandam to her self's confusion.
> For, as an old, rude, rotten, tune-less Kit,
> *If famous Dowland daign to finger it,*
> Makes sweeter Musick then the choisest Lute
> In the grosse handling of a clownish Brute:[9]

The third section, "The Furies," describes the dire results of the Fall as it affected Adam and Eve and changed the nature of the world. The furies are represented by the discords wrought by Sin: Sickness, War, Famine, and the destructive Passions man is now heir to. These were the conventional medieval didactic materials so familiar in treatises on the Seven Deadly Sins. The fourth section, "The Handy-Crafts," describes the condition of Adam and Eve after their expulsion from Paradise, tells the story of Cain and Abel, and catalogues various inventions of mankind, such as the taming of the horse and the forging of iron. The marginal note at line 568 comments: "While Cain and his children are busie for the world, *Adam* & his other sons exercise themselves in piety and justice, and in searching the godly secrets of Nature." Du Bartas thus managed to introduce a further extended passage of devotional commentary by having Adam instruct his son Seth in the theological problems of Creation, the Fall, the promised Redemption, and the present state of the world—a résumé, in effect, of the very material which the poet planned to cover.

It is evident, from these last two sections, that the material is neither heroic in nature nor sufficiently related to the narrative to be taken as episodes in unified development. Du Bartas took seriously the view of the didactic purpose of the epic and made his instruction encyclopedic in range, though he violated the principle of decorum outrageously. For example, after having harrowed the reader with a description of Cain's murder of Abel, he briskly proceeded to describe early housebuilding in the most homely terms:

> One fels down Firs, another of the same
> With crosséd Poles a little lodge doth frame:
> Another mounds it with dry wals about
> (And leaves a breach for passage in and out)
> With Turf and Furse: some others yet more gross
> Their homely Sties in stead of wals inclose:
> Some (like the Swallow) mud and hay do mix,
> And that about their silly Cotes they fix:
> Some make their roofs with fearn, or reeds, or rushes
> And some with hides, with oase, with boughs, and bushes.[10]

Sylvester's diction reminds one curiously of Wordsworth's early attempts to approximate the speech of common men.

It is probably quite unfair to Du Bartas and to Sylvester to comment on the lack of classical form, for, as Du Bartas himself wrote, his *Second Weeke* was not purely epic or heroic, but in part panegyric, in part prophetic, and in part didactic. What is important, however, is that Du Bartas was actually considering the epic design inherent in the Christian view of universal history. Yet the very fact that he organized his material on a chronological basis suggests that he had not fully grasped the dramatic unity implicit in the material itself. The invocations, the devotional comments, and the constant use of figural interpretation are evidence that he recognized Christ as the central event in Christian history: but the fact that he proposed to treat of the Messias in a single "day," after allotting a day each to Adam, Noah, Abraham, David, and Zedechiah, indicates a disregard of, or failure to perceive, dramatic proportions. In the chronological arrangement, Christ would have come as a climax to the history of the Old Testament, but would not have been so dramatically the turning point of the whole Christian epic design.

We can only speculate upon how Du Bartas would have dealt with the figure of Christ had he lived to complete the work. In his treatment of the history of David in the Fourth Day he had moved somewhat away from the discursive and devotional style of the earlier parts to a more direct paraphrastic style, particularly in the accounts of warlike actions. He still indulged in many digressions into commentary material, as in his explanation of Satan's role in Saul's recourse to the witch of Endor,[11] but he showed a greater willingness to let the Bible account stand unembellished where the narrative element was dominant. In treating the life of Christ, Du Bartas would probably have followed a chronological pattern and very likely would have divided his "day" into four parts corresponding to the traditional devotional emphasis upon the Incarnation, the Temptation, the Passion, and the Resurrection. There is no indication that he conceived the life of Christ as heroic in a classical sense or that he would have stressed the human life and teachings of Christ rather than the theological and doctrinal significance.

If we accept Du Bartas's own description of the *Divine Weekes* as part epic, part panegyric, part prophetic, and part didactic, we shall probably have a better sense of the various elements which the poet saw fit to combine in the work. The epic element lies chiefly in the magnitude of the design, but is supported by obvious classical epic features and imitations of Homer or Virgil. There is, for example, a parallel between the proposition and invocation of Du Bartas's *Second Weeke,* First Day, and the opening lines of Virgil's *Aeneid* in which the cause of calamity is questioned:

> . . . tell me what mis-deed
> Banisht both *Eden's Adam,* and his seed:
> Tell who (immortall) mortalizing, brought us
> The Balm from heav'n which hopéd health hath wrought us:
> Grant me the story of the Church to sing,
> And gests of Kings: Let me this Totall bring
> From thy first Sabbath to his fatall Toomb,
> My stile extending to the Day of Doome.[12]

The whole scope of the Christian epic is here outlined and the role of Christ, immortal "mortalizing," made central. Although the poet particularizes his subject in the words "Church" and "gests of Kings," his real theme is the fortunes of mankind from the Fall to the Day of Judgment. There is another parallel between Du Bartas's Christian story of the Fall and Virgil's account of the enmity of Juno for the Trojan progenitors of Rome. Satan's hatred for the new race of beings and Juno's for Aeneas had been compared in the traditional moralizing of the *Aeneid,*

and it is hard to conceive that Du Bartas was unaware of such
"epic" similarities. His description of the "sundry subtle and
horrible endeavors of the Divell, putting on divers forms to
overthrow man-kinde,"[13] and the general forms in which evil
angels seduce the race of men[14] suggests Dryden's later conception of supernatural machines based on the Biblical accounts of
the good and bad angels.

The panegyric element consists not only in the praise of the
great personages of the Bible but also in many digressions laud-
ing famous men throughout history. Both Du Bartas and Sylvester were full of praise for their respective monarchs, Henry
IV and James I, and Sylvester's English pride in his own nation's
history is continually made evident. Time and again Sylvester
draws his own comparisons with events in the history of England and develops the theme that the country will know peace
and glory only when united under the God-appointed prince.
The patriotic note is especially strong in Sylvester's execration
of the Gunpowder Plot of 1605, in which the relationship of
"Prince, Peers, and People" is considered as a kind of parallel
to the troubles of David's reign.[15]

The didactic element is so evident that there is little need to
point out examples; whole sections such as "Babylon" and "Col-
onies" (*Second Weeke,* Second Day) are devoted to classifica-
tions of languages and races in an encyclopedic fashion, and
traditional exegetical materials can be found upon nearly every
page. The "Propheticall" part, however, is worth consideration.
There can be little doubt that Du Bartas was referring to both
the prophecies of Christ in the Old Testament and the larger
promise for the race of man assured by the Atonement and the
Redemption. In this sense he was concerned with the whole
design of the Christian epic action. He used figural interpretation constantly, as in this comment on the significance of
Manna:

> O Israel! see in this Table-pure,
> In this fair glasse, thy Saviour's portrayture,
> The Son of God, MESSIAS promised,
> The sacred seed, to bruise the Serpent's head:[16]

His plan to devote the last two days of the *Second Weeke* to Christ and to the Eternal Sabbath, however, suggests that his real interest was in the theological significance of the Redemption. For Du Bartas, prophecy was essentially a theological matter, the subject for devotional commentary, rather than an epic device. There is, of course, a parallel between the classical sense of destiny and the Christian faith in God's foreordained Eternal Sabbath, but it is doubtful that Du Bartas considered such similarities applicable to his project. He was always careful to distinguish between the truth of Christian faith and the error of pagan fables; he made references to pagan myths, but, as he explained, he did so "par métonomie" and left no doubt that they were dubious fictions.

The *Divine Weekes,* then, though reflecting the Renaissance interest in classical literature, remained essentially a Protestant compendium of traditional medieval encyclopedic lore and hexameral exegesis. The fact that Du Bartas had adopted a strictly classical form modeled on Virgil's for his *Judith* (1565) before he began work on the *Divine Weekes* indicates that his choice of the discursive form for the hexameral subjects was deliberate. His real enthusiasm was for the didactic and devotional elements. The subject of the *First Weeke,* the seven days of Creation, could hardly be viewed as heroic matter, though it implied the "epic" view of universal history. In the *Second Weeke,* however, the Christian epic theme was far more explicit, and it is not surprising, therefore, that it shows greater evidence of Du Bartas's awareness of classical parallels and heroic features. Yet he apparently regarded the epic elements as secondary to the didactic and prophetic, and had no desire to abandon his discursive form for a classical one. An interesting comment on his treatment of David is provided by the scholar Simon Goulart de Senlis, who supplied summaries, notes, and commentary to the complete edition of Du Bartas in the Chouet text (Paris, 1589).

En ces chapitres, le S. Esprit nous fait voir les merveilles de Dieu en l'infirmité de son serviteur David. Le Poète représente les principaux poincts d'icelle histoire en onze cens vers ou environs, choisissant ce qui lui a semblé plus digne d'estre compris en l'œuvre par lui entrepris. Car une Davideide vaudroit bien le cours d'une Enéide, ou le nombre des livres de l'Iliade et l'Odyssée ensemble si quelque Chrestien et docte poète François vouloit y employer le temps et l'estude, comme un si noble et fertile sujet le mérite. Mais le Sieur du Bartas, qui ne vouloit ainsi s'estendre, ains visoit à se maintenir en sa bienséance accoustumée, s'est convenablement enclos en ce cercle d'un petit nombre de vers, qui comprenent une infinité de choses, sous le nom de *Trophées* ou marques des victoires de David; que nous rapportons à quatre principaux.[17]

Thus, in the view of a contemporary of Du Bartas, a full-scale classical epic could be made of the subject of David, but the poet preferred to treat the material in his accustomed discursive manner. It is interesting to note that Cowley later planned his *Davideis* almost exactly on Goulart's pattern, and it is not unreasonable to suppose that he may have read the scholar's commentary.

In connection with hexameral materials, the Assembly in Hell received special development. Genesis tells only the subtlety of the serpent in the temptation of Eve, but Christian exegesis had very early introduced the identification with Satan and his enmity toward God's newly created race of beings. The conflict between good and evil was thus dramatized in a universal setting, and the figure of Satan, or Lucifer, the angelic bearer of light fallen through pride, became an inseparable part of the hexameral story. Even today, few people reared in the Christian

tradition can read Genesis without automatically assuming the
malice of the devil to be working through the serpent. The
history of the Christian concept of Satan is too complex to be
discussed here, but it is clear that in the Middle Ages Satan and
his hordes became stock literary figures in saints' lives, treatises
on sin, and mystery plays. Contempt for the world meant contempt for the flesh and the devil also. Contempt could be expressed in both serious and humorous fashion, as the grotesques
and the comic Vice attest. The traditional view is well expressed
in the following passage from St. Athanasius' *Life of St. Anthony (ca.* 357):

When the prince of demons appears like this, the crafty one, he tries
to strike terror by speaking great things, as the Lord revealed to Job,
"he counteth iron as straw, and brass as rotten wood, yea he counteth
the sea as a pot of ointment, and the depth of the abyss as a captive
and the abyss as a covered walk" (Job xli. 18ff.).... Such are their
boasts and professions that they may deceive the godly. But not even
then ought we, the faithful, to fear his appearance or give heed to his
words. For he is a liar and speaketh of truth never a word. In spite
of his big words and his enormous boldness, there is no doubt he was
drawn with a hook by the Saviour, and as a beast of burden he had
his nostrils bored through with stakes, and as a runaway he was
dragged by the ring in his nose, and his tongue was tied with a cord
(Job xl. 19ff.). And he was bound by the Lord as a sparrow, that we
should mock at him.[18]

Satan's role in the Christian epic, then, was well established,
and the imaginative concept of Satan presiding over an infernal
council, plotting revenge, was a natural development. M. W.
Bloomfield[19] cites an example of the literary use of the infernal
council from about 1430, *A Song Called the Devil's Parliament*
(MS Lambeth 853). A consultation of devils takes place at Jesus'
birth in order to plan countermeasures to this great threat, and
the chief devil undertakes to tempt Jesus with the Seven Deadly

Sins. He has, of course, no more success with the temptation than all the devils later have in resisting the Harrowing of Hell by Christ. The Old English poem *Christ and Satan* is an even clearer portrayal of Satan's failure to tempt Christ and of the relationship of Satan and his followers in Hell. In these poems, the setting of universal history and the hexameral themes of Creation and the Fall (often with a survey to Doomsday) all serve to make Christ the central figure, and the contest with Satan the climax of the divine drama.

To judge by the frequency of the appearance of an infernal council in narrative works before Milton, we must conclude that it was something of a set piece which could be employed, as in Phineas Fletcher's *Apollyonists,* apart from the conventional hexameral setting. In the *Devils' Parliament* and in *Christ and Satan,* the infernal council is called to meet the threat of Christ. In Vida's *Christiad* there are three such scenes in Hell. Du Bartas, in describing Satan's temptation of Eve, did not elaborate upon an infernal council, but he did comment on the nature and disguises of the horde of lesser devils.[20] In the visit of Saul to the witch at Endor, Du Bartas pictured the shade of Samuel as really the disguise of Satan, and again discoursed upon the power of the devils to work through confused minds. In allegorical form, the hosts of Hell plot against and besiege the "Isle of Man" in Phineas Fletcher's *Purple Island*. Crashaw's translation from Marino, *The Suspicion of Herod* (1644), opens with an infernal council in which Satan recounts their enmity toward God and man and appoints Cruelty to tempt Herod to the slaying of the children in hopes of destroying Christ. Cowley adopted the device at the beginning of the *Davideis,* describing Satan's speech to the assembled devils and his dispatch of Envy in the shape of Benjamin to promote Saul's hatred of David.

The infernal council was but an elaboration of the device of using Satan as a kind of supernatural machine. It could be applied both to Biblical subjects and, in the fashion of the morality play, to any situation in which the cause of vice might be explained in the dramatic context of universal history. Its Christian roots lie in the Biblical accounts of Satan's enmity, particularly in the Book of Job, in the hexameral elaboration of the fall from Heaven and the temptation of Adam and Eve, and in the medieval portrayal of the devil at work in the world. The descriptions of Christ's Harrowing of Hell might be considered as contributing to the general picture. There can be little doubt that the scenes in Hell were regarded as providing much the same epic effect as Ulysses' visit to Hades (*Odyssey*, Book XI) or Aeneas' journey to the underworld (*Aeneid*, Book VI) and that Satan's machinations were highly effective counterparts of the pagan supernatural.

Discussing the use of Christian *merveilleux* in the French Biblical epics, Professor Sayce points out: "The most important for the epic were those which concerned angels and demons, the powers of Heaven and the powers of Hell. The importance attached to them is again simply explained: they correspond to the conflicting forces of gods and goddesses in classical epics."[21] Among many examples, he cites Coras's *David,* in which Satan and the archangel Michael are portrayed as the supernatural helpers of Goliath and of David, respectively. In the same poem, a demon akin to a classical Fury brings about Saul's madness. In Desmarets's *Esther,* Lucifer plans the destruction of the Jews, but must submit to the arbitrary limitations imposed upon his work of temptation by the archangel Michael. The restriction of Satan's power was, of course, authorized by the example of the Book of Job, in which God limits the Adversary. But, as Professor Sayce points out, there was a weakness inherent in the use of the Christian marvelous: "In the classical epic the struggle between the gods was waged on equal terms. Here the conflict is illusory, since one camp can only operate within the limits set

by the other. Theological appearances are saved at the expense
of the poetic effect."[22]

When the French and English Biblical epic poets contrived
marvelous elements in artificial imitation of classical parallels,
they were open to the charge of such critics as Boileau that their
wonders were either dull or ridiculous, and degraded Christianity. Nevertheless, the use of angels and demons as the chief
elements in the Christian marvelous was a well-established con-
vention. Cowley provided scenes in Heaven and speeches by
God, and used angels as messengers and bearers of prophetic
visions; clearly he thought it suitable to construct Christian epic
machines along the lines of the classical. In a note to Book II he
speaks of the fates, "that is, according to the Christian Poetical
manner of speaking, the Angels, to whom the Government of
this World is committed."[23] The hexameral materials thus possessed elements which were developed along the lines of the classical epic; the role of Satan as the Adversary of God and man
was particularly suitable for epic treatment and had already been
associated with the epic before Milton made it so dramatic a part
of his grand design.

The other hexameral works of the period were close imitations
of Du Bartas and Sylvester. Sir William Alexander's *Doomes-day*
(1614) was probably conceived as a counterpart to Du Bartas's
Creation, covering as it does much the same material of universal
history but, as it were, in retrospect. The work is immensely
prolix, running to over eleven thousand lines, an average of 112
eight-line stanzas for each of the twelve books or "Houres." In
one sense the work is not really a narrative but an accumulation
of devotional thoughts and moral examples in the medieval style.
The first "Houre" does, however, provide a rapid narrative of
the chief events of universal history from the Creation and Fall
to the Day of Judgment. The next two "Houres" describe the
preparation for Doomsday and the signs which will precede it.

The fourth "Houre" describes the rising of the dead from the earth, and the fifth begins the judgment of the assembled souls. From then on, Alexander treats the various kinds of sinners and their just punishment, and contrasts them with the assembly of saints. The eighth "Houre" is devoted to the patriarchs, kings, and prophets who "Yet did but Christ by Types and figures see."[24] As in Du Bartas, the design of the Christian epic is there, but the whole is suffocated by devotional piety. The measured judgment of the work's most recent editors, L. E. Kastner and H. B. Charlton, will suffice to round out this description:

> The general material of the poem is inert; it does not of itself fall into such lines as would unmistakably suggest to the poet the pattern of an organic structure. Of architecture, therefore, there is none beyond a simple framework, and into it Alexander packs the heavy mass of his opinions on sin and his tedious exhortations to take the orthodox way for circumventing the everlasting bonfire. Even narrative appears but episodically, and the poem is less the telling of a story then the marshalling of a procession. At a point here or there—the final destruction of one or other of God's creatures, for instance, or the dawning of the day of wrath itself—there is matter for effective description. But Alexander's imagination is not apt for such great occasions, and he merely weakens traditional renderings by drawing them more lengthily out.[25]

Thomas Peyton's *Glasse of Time* (1620, 1623) was a very serious imitation of Du Bartas by a very serious gentleman of Lincoln's Inn. Peyton's primary purpose in undertaking his hexameral narrative was apparently to unburden his soul of many troubling thoughts, the chief of which was his passionate conviction that the Sabbath was no longer properly observed. The narrative base, consisting of the Fall of Adam and Eve and the fortunes of their progeny to Noah, with reminders of Doomsday along the way, was but a tenuous thread holding large discursive fragments together. The digressions, which Peyton freely confessed in such lines as: "And back to Adam whence I last digrest,"[20] were concerned with almost everything from a violent attack upon the Pope to such exegetical questions as where Paradise was located, why there were different colored races of men, what became of Cain's descendants, and so forth. Often he simply listed the commentary authorities and offered no real conclusion but a general moral one.[27] Sometimes the Biblical situation suggested a parallel in contemporary events or recent history, such as Geneva beset by the Catholic alliance of France, Spain, and the Pope. The narrative was continually broken by addresses to his Muse, Urania, and moral exhortations to the reader, often in the form of rhetorical questions.

Peyton had even less sense of the heroic than Alexander, although he contrived for himself and his endeavor an air of profound solemnity at the beginning. Once under way, however, he became a garrulous chatterer, continually reminding himself of his purpose and ostentatiously pulling himself back to the thread of his narrative. Where Du Bartas and later Milton were concerned with the profound wonder of the Creation, Peyton was primarily intrigued by the question why God rested on the seventh day. This led him to a long digression about the proper Christian observation of the Sabbath to which he devoted almost a third of the first book. The first book concluded with a rather obscure, semiallegorical representation of the debate between Justice and Mercy in a curious emblematic setting modeled on an engraving of the Gates of Paradise.

Peyton, apparently, was open to influence from any number of sources. Although he covered much the same material as Du Bartas and Milton, he does not belong in the group of narrative poets who were moving toward the classical form. Nor does he belong to the older medieval tradition in all respects. He was essentially a devotional poet who, lacking a consistent guiding principle in his writing, adopted conventional forms of heroic poems, sermons, and pious treatises, but half-remembered, and proceeded on the strength of his convictions and his interests to concoct an instructive poem. The personal nature of his writing is nowhere more evident than in the rather pathetic account, at the beginning of his second book, of his own misfortunes—ruined by slander, treachery, and cunning. Although he suffered many trials, his response was not heroic, nor was his fortitude confirmed. His theme was the age-old one of finding in the universal condition the weaknesses of his own situation. His work is evidence, nevertheless, of both the popularity of the hexameral materials and the strength of the religious habit of viewing the individual in the universal context.

In all the hexameral works noted here, the devotional element tends to dominate the narrative and to make the interest in the action of the temptation and Fall of Adam and Eve secondary to the interest in the theological and moral significance. A triangular relationship is set up, the three corners of which are Adam, Christ, and the reader. The story of the first Fall and its consequences is the base, but the devotional commentary makes explicit the warning to the reader whose soul is in danger and whose only hope lies in faith in Christ's act of Redemption.

The Doomsday works are emphatic about the grief and pain of the sinner at the Last Judgment, and the unspeakable joys that await the pilgrim soul attaining salvation through trial and suffering. Sir William Mure's *Doomesday* (1628) is hardly a narrative poem, but it provides many examples of the imagery of temptation, fall, repentance, suffering, and reward and punishment. In a fervent but strained apostrophe, Mure addressed the soul that had attained Heaven's bliss:

> But O! when Thou casts back thine eyes,
> Thy voyage dangerous espyes,
> Foes and ambushments, laide to surprise
>   Thy wayes, when thou dost vieu;

The traines set foorth Thee to entise,
Base pleasures, which Thou didst despise,
What boundlesse joyes shall thence arise,
    What solace sweet ensue?[28]

The soul thus addressed is in a sense the reader's, but it is also the abstract and ideal Christian soul acting in the vast impersonal context of the cosmos and of universal history, and seeking to find its way in relation to the two main points of reference, Adam and Christ.

CHAPTER III

OLD TESTAMENT HEROIC POETRY

ALTHOUGH rapid surveys or paraphrases of Old Testament history were often appended to the hexameral materials as part of the view of universal history, they should be kept distinct from those that developed in the first half of the seventeenth century from a special interest in the stories and personages of the Old Testament as potential heroic narrative subjects. The hexameral materials provided the religious poets with a vast framework for a display of devotion and learning, but the very universality of the design created a context in which human actions were measured according to the way they represented aspects of the cosmic conflict rather than by their own dramatic qualities. In such a setting, the Old Testament heroes were viewed primarily as types and figures of theological or moral significance, and only secondarily as individuals with well-defined human qualities.

The devotional practice of calling to mind a series of such figures as analogies was so widespread and habitual that examples can be found throughout the religious poetry of the period. Traditional exegesis had gone a certain way toward embellishing Biblical figures and incidents such as those of Noah and the Flood, and in the medieval mystery plays and paraphrases many more touches of an imaginative nature crept in to individualize such figures as Noah's wife or the shepherd Mak. In Du Bartas's *Second Weeke* there is evidence that the poet became interested in the human problems of Joseph, Moses, Jephthah, and David, for he expanded the narrative element, but for the most part he was concerned with the devotional elements. Within the vast design of universal history, he could not afford to give too much attention to any one figure, but within

[53]

the more restricted scope of his heroic poem *Judith* he felt free to expand and embellish the subject in a very different way.

There was an unmistakable correlation between the interest in Old Testament materials and the interest in heroic poetry as it developed a closer approximation to classical form. For a time the Old Testament heroes seemed to provide the closest parallels to the classical epic heroes. Such parallels as those of Hercules and Samson had long been established in the commentaries and in the moralization of the classical epics, and, even at the end of the seventeenth century, pagan mythology was still considered by some to be an obscure perversion of the ancient Hebrew truths. In practice, however, very few of the Old Testament stories and figures could sustain the interest required for a full-scale epic. The subject of David, with the wealth of historical material associated with him, probably had the greatest potential, but even Cowley, who had planned the most ambitious design for his *Davideis,* apparently lost interest and soon abandoned his project.

If the Old Testament failed to provide the ideal subject for a Christian epic modeled on clasical form, it nevertheless constituted for the Biblical narrative poets of the first half of the century the main source of material. The Hebraic morality, with its well-defined sense of sin, the sense of being called or chosen of God, and the sense of direct inspiration by God, had a special appeal for the Protestants of that age. Since the heroic poem's primary purpose was conceived to be moral instruction, setting forth historical examples of valor and virtue, the Old Testament, read in the light of the New, seemed to offer the best source of historical examples of Christian heroic morality. Other major sources were the medieval saints' lives and the martyrologies, but these were rejected by Protestants as being too closely associated with Catholicism. Foxe's *Book of Martyrs* might have provided some material, but it was perhaps too

recent to possess the universal and timeless qualities often considered necessary for the heroic poem. The choice, then, was
either to experiment with Biblical subjects or to turn, like
Ariosto and Spenser, to the embellishment of history or legend
with a Christian allegory or fable appropriate to the moral purpose. By the middle of the century, Davenant and Hobbes were
arguing for the latter course, but in the first half of the century
the major interest was centered upon the Old Testament.

It was not to be expected that the religious poets would
wholly compromise their primary interest in Christian themes
in order to imitate slavishly the classical models. The concept of
a Christian kind of heroism was bound to prevail, even though
an attempt was made to imitate classical structure and epic devices. The essentially Christian concern with the problem of a
moral choice, with the trial and suffering attendant upon the
conflict of vice and virtue, and with the moral triumph of the
hero who, through the influence of grace, exemplifies the pattern
for the salvation of the individual soul, characterizes most of
the Biblical narratives in the first half of the century. For the
Protestant in particular, it was the struggle of the soul to achieve
a personal sense of salvation which put the emphasis upon the
heroism of choice and trial. The Old Testament figures exemplified also a direct relationship between God and man, and a
clear-cut morality determined by the Will of God, which had
a special appropriateness in terms of Protestant doctrine. Furthermore, the fact that the Old Testament figures had historical
reality and were true as presented in the Word of God made
them appear far superior to both the classical pagan heroes and
the heroes of the allegorical romances.

Christianity had traditionally associated suffering with temptation and moral choice. Sin and suffering had come into the
world as a result of the first Temptation and Fall in the Garden
of Eden. Subsequent human suffering could thus be interpreted

in two ways: either as retribution and punishment for the wrong moral choice, or as sacrifice for the cause of the right. The latter was obviously a form of heroism which could be viewed as parallel to the sufferings of Christ for the redemption of mankind. The Church thus tended to give the temptations and trials of the saints and martyrs both a moral and a mystical interpretation, elaborating the latter with legends of miracles and conflicts with demons and evil spirits. Protestantism tended to reject the emphasis upon the miraculous and the supernatural, but retained the stress upon moral choice and personal faith. The Old Testament figures were preferred as true historical examples of Christian heroism and morality.

The fact that Christ was always the ultimate point of reference strengthened the specifically Christian aspects of the morality and gave special meaning to the examples of trial, suffering, and sacrifice. The Old Testament, however, had its own Hebraic morality which stressed justice in terms of the Law, and punishment and suffering as direct consequences of sin. Theologically, Christ represented the supreme act of Divine Mercy, an overcoming of the inexorable decrees of Divine Justice by means of a mystical Atonement. The Hebraic and Christian sense of sin, therefore, never allowed the concept of suffering as a retribution for sin to die out, even though the New Testament had established Christ as the bringer of a new moral dispensation of mercy and love. The Protestant poet tended to treat the theme of Divine Mercy in devotional or doctrinal form and to emphasize the theme of Divine Justice in the portrayal of moral action. When he turned to the Old Testament for subject matter, he naturally found few examples of mercy in the Christian sense, but he did find an abundance of examples of right or wrong moral choice. As a result, the majority of Old Testament subjects in the heroic narrative poetry of the first half of the century exemplify trial, temptation, suffering as a consequence of sin, and the heroism of virtue or faith triumphant.

The concept of Christian heroism was thus a combination of many elements: the traditional stress upon the mystical and moral significance of trial and suffering, the Hebraic concern with sin and its consequences, the humanist interest in nobility of character, and the Protestant emphasis upon individual responsibility for moral choice. Such a concept of heroism made the world the main arena of action, and morality the chief measure of the hero. Strength of faith was perhaps the ultimate measure, but faith required convincing demonstration in active moral terms. Even the patience of Job when confronted by unexplainable suffering could be viewed as a demonstration of moral fortitude as well as strength of faith. Job was no helpless martyr but an exemplar of righteous indignation in a situation in which the basic principles of justice were perversely interpreted and undermined by Job's friends. For Protestants, the direct relationship between God and Job made the moral aspects of the problem especially significant; the Book of Job was the profoundly moving study of the individual soul's responsibility both to choose rightly and to hold fast through terrible trial.

When the religious poets turned to the classical epics for models of heroic poetry, they found very few examples among the classical heroes that wholly fitted a concept of Christian heroism. None of Homer's protagonsists is tested in a significantly moral way, and Virgil's Aeneas is made to undergo trials of a moral sort only in the opening books; by the sixth book he has become an instrument of Fate, impelled to the task put upon him. Of the classical heroes well known in the Renaissance, Hercules was most clearly seen as a moral figure. As Professor Hallett Smith has shown,[1] the legend of Hercules' choice be-

---

[1] For notes to chapter iii see page 144.

tween vice and virtue was popular, and his twelve labors had long been moralized as representative of the victory over fleshly desires and temptations. Hercules' subduing of Antaeus was interpreted by Fulgentius as the conquest of lust. As a model of heroism, however, Hercules lacked the prestige he would have had if he had been the subject of a great classical epic.

Although there are many similarities between the classical and the Christian view of the valour and nobility of the heroic protagonist, Christian morality and classical pagan morality differed in basic ways. In the world through which the classical hero moved, inexorable and unknowable Fate transcended even the gods, yet the world was subject to the local interference of elemental deities and supernatural forces. In such a world the classical hero was measured by his ability to assert his courage and fortitude in spite of the chance buffets of Fate. The Old Testament hero pursued his way in a world in which the Will of God was always operative and history was interpreted as a direct relationship between God and man. Such a world was less open to supernatural whimsicalities and more representative of a Divine Plan working in the affairs of men.

Both worlds have parallels in their oracles and prophecies, emphasizing Fate or Divine Will. Of the two, however, the Old Testament prophecy was far less ambiguous and more directly and concretely applicable. Aeneas was informed of his appointed task, but he could not always be sure that it was not a trick of some antagonistic god. Moses also had moments of doubt and uncertainty, but he knew that he could not escape from his task. Furthermore, Old Testament prophecy often involved a moral choice. Even in the earliest legends and myths of the Israelites, the man of God is subjected to a testing of his faith and character: Noah, Abraham and Isaac, Lot, Joseph and Potiphar's wife, Moses in the wilderness, and, of course, the original and primal temptation of Adam and Eve. In the later, more historical books, the choice was often a matter of morality and faith in combination, not, as with Hercules, simply a test of virtue and strength. Saul's failure to adhere completely to God's command-ment to destroy all of Amalek and its riches was the reason for the rejection of Saul as king. The moral degeneration of Saul followed as a natural consequence. David's sin with Bathsheba and the murder of Uriah required heartfelt repentance before God and man were reconciled.

The world in which Aeneas was appointed by Fate to found Rome was one in which suffering was not so clearly a matter of personal trial or choice, or even of punishment for sin. Before the final triumph over Turnus, Aeneas could justly take pride in his courage and fortitude, but he was equally justified in con-cluding that he was the unluckiest of men. The machinations of the rival gods as they affected the fortunes of the hero had no immediate relationship to the inexorable working out of Fate. The Old Testament writers had a much stronger sense of the direct relationship between God's will and human actions. There is no doubt that the classical hero suffered many trials in the course of his life, but his sufferings are incidental to the task he is impelled to undertake. Aeneas' state of mind as he witnesses and takes part in the final agonies of Troy has little of the Job-like quality. His courage is fully displayed and his qualifica-tions for leadership are demonstrated, but his anguish in this situation serves primarily to emphasize the horror of Troy's destruction. Much of his subsequent suffering is the result of the back-stage rivalry of the supernatural hierarchy; perhaps only in his decision to leave Dido does Aeneas illustrate a sig-nificant moral choice.

The important difference between the Christian concept of heroism and classical heroism is demonstrated in the treatment of human suffering and the emphasis upon moral choice. It is not surprising that the religious poets should choose from the

possible Old Testament heroic figures those which illustrate
trials involving moral issues. A few figures could be viewed as
classical types of heroes, particularly those engaged in war and
conquest — actions involving courage, nobility, or prowess in
battle. In this group would fall the stories of Judith, David and
Goliath, Samson (as champion), and Saul and Jonathan. These
few, significantly, are the only ones treated in heroic fashion in
the first half of the century. Joshua or Gideon would seem to be
obvious choices, and had been considered heroic in the Middle
Ages, but there is no evidence that any of the narrative poets of
the seventeenth century considered them heroic subjects.

In contrast, the Old Testament stories and protagonists that
illustrate the heroism of moral trial and suffering are over-
whelmingly in the majority. The temptation of Joseph was
treated by Sylvester, Aylett, and Boyd. The Book of Job was a
subject for Sylvester, Quarles, and Sandys; the first two stressed
the heroic and triumphant elements. The story of Jonah, with
its two-sided moral application, was treated by Quarles and
Boyd. David's sin with Bathsheba, unheroic though it was, became the subject of heroic narratives by Sabie and Fuller, and
would undoubtedly have been fully treated by Cowley had he
completed the *Davideis*. The anonymous poem *David's Troubles
Remembered* (1638) focused on the same incident. Aylett developed a poem of over three thousand lines on Susanna and
the moral trial of the elders. And, of course, Milton conceived
of Samson as heroic in the realm of faith and moral resolution,
though sorely tempted and suffering.

From such a conception of spiritual and moral trial in the
purely human realm, it is not very far to Milton's conception
of Christ in *Paradise Regained* as the ultimate example of the
way in which the human soul can resist the supreme temptations of the world and its glories. Milton's Christ rejects all
those things which for the classical hero would be the greatest

accomplishments, not only worldly power and glory but also, much more seductive, knowledge and wisdom in the classical or humanist sense. With Milton, then, the concept of the Christian hero comes ultimately to Christ himself; the Old Testament figures could be treated as examples of moral trial and choice, but they remained shadowy or imperfect types of Christ or of the Christian dispensation. Their main advantage for the narrative poet was that they were human examples traditionally considered in terms of Christian morality.

Du Bartas's *Judith*, translated by both Thomas Hudson and Sylvester, was the earliest example and the chief model of the Biblical heroic poem for the English narrative poets. Since Professor Tillyard has given the poem in the Sylvester translation a thorough analysis in his recent book,[2] it is unnecessary to do more than point to some of its main features. The accounts of the siege, the narrated stories of war and conquest, and the description of the destruction of Holofernes' army are heroic in nature. But much of the poem is given over to Puritan social and moral comment. Judith is portrayed as a model of Puritan womanhood, trained in the strictest morality (Books II, IV). Holofernes is pictured as an almost comic example of immoderate lust, gluttony, and drunkenness (Books V, VI). There is perhaps an element of inner conflict before Judith decides her course of action, but the decision is made primarily because the wind has opened her Bible to the story of Sisera and Jael. She undergoes a bad moment of fear and irresolution just before she delivers the fatal blow, but a fervent prayer to God gives her the power:

> O, let it land: with *Poppie's* sleepiest sap
> This Tyrant's sense benum in end-lesse Nap;
> That I may raise this Siege, Thy Thralls release,
> Return Thee *Praise*; and to Thy SION, *Peace*.[3]

The poem fittingly closes with a hymn sung by Judith and the Hebrew women, emphasizing God's justice in bringing low the tyrant who has scorned the power of true faith.

Drayton's *Moses His Birth and Miracles* (1604) was influenced by Du Bartas and Sylvester, for the poet addressed them directly in the opening lines. Drayton may have been aware also of a French poem on the same subject: Christophe de Gamon's *Les Playes de l'Egypte,* printed in *Le Verger Poetique* (Lyons, 1597).⁴ Although Drayton's *Moses* is about the same length as the *Judith,* divided into three books, it is as much a chronicle as a heroic poem. Drayton's interest lay in description and in learned embellishment. The first book recounts the birth of Moses, his finding and raising by Termuth, and his brief term of favor with Pharaoh. Drayton pictures Moses as leading the Egyptian army to victory against the invading Ethiopians, but he does not make much of the heroic action. In the second book, however, is a detailed account of each of the ten plagues, part descriptive and part learned. Drayton gives a clue to his close interest in the subject in the following digression:

> Afflicted *London,* in sixe hundred three,
> When God thy sinne so grievously did strike,
> And from th' infection that did spring from thee,
> The spacious Ile was patient of the like.
> That sickly season, when I undertooke
> This composition faintly to supply,
> When thy afflictions serv'd me for a booke,
> Whereby to modell Egypts miserie . . .⁵

Drayton obviously viewed his poem as instructive for the people of his own time, for in the third book he provided a further contemporary analogy to emphasize God's justice in destroying the Egyptian army in the Red Sea:

> In eightie eight at *Dover* that had beene,
> To view that Navie (like a mighty wood)

Whose sailes swept Heaven, might eas'lie there have seene,
How puissant *Pharaoh* perish'd in the floud.
What for a conquest strictly they did keepe,
Into the channell presently was pour'd,
Castilian riches scattered on the deepe,
That *Spaines* long hopes had sodainly devour'd.
The afflicted English rang'd along the strand
To waite what would this threatning power betide,
Now when the Lord with a victorious hand
In his high justice scourg'd the *Iberian* pride.[8]

The poem is a good example of the way in which heroic devices were adopted from classical models to embellish a narrative whose prime purpose was not devotional or theological but rather moral application with social and national overtones. Even the conventional figural interpretation is absent, and the story is presented with an almost bare directness. It is only in the passages where Drayton could give colorful description, as in the account of Termuth's walk by the Nile or the catalogues of the plagues in the second book, that he allowed his poetic fancy free play.

Drayton's later and shorter poem, *David and Golia* (1630), shows a greater interest in the heroic element with its accounts of the armies, the color and activity of the camps and soldiers, and the dramatic scene of David's victory. It ends so abruptly that it hardly seems a complete poem in itself, but rather a fragment of a larger epic design. There is no indication that Drayton was contemplating a full-scale epic poem on David, but the opening lines suggest that he had a more extensive treatment in mind than the brief narrative which he completed. The last lines, with the concluding brusque phrase, "where 'tis time I leave," further suggest that Drayton had intended to go on, but for some unknown reason decided to stop abruptly and unceremoniously. In view of Cowley's abandonment of his plans, one must tentatively conclude that epic designs on the subject of

David were usually doomed by an early failure of poetic enthusiasm. Perhaps the subject of David, in the last analysis, simply
did not provide the stimulation necessary to sustain the effort
of the poet. Possibly the scope of David's life, though including
a number of potentially heroic or moral incidents, was too diffuse
to be managed in a unified and consistent manner. The Bible
account was essentially a chronicle history in which the figure
of David assumed different forms and meanings: shepherd boy,
youthful champion, singer, psalmist, king, sinner, repentant
servant of God, unhappy father, and, of course, figurally of the
seed from which Christ sprang.

It is not surprising that the dramatic or narrative poets tended
to select significant aspects from the life of David rather than
undertake the whole. Nor, in view of the interest in heroism
involving temptation and trial, is it surprising that the incident
of David's adultery with Bathsheba should be one of the most
popular. Yet this subject was more suitable for devotional moralizing than for heroic narrative. Sabie had adopted some heroic
devices to embellish his poem, but he had made unmistakable
the fact that David was a moral example. Thomas Fuller, in his
three poems on David,[7] left no doubt that his purpose was devotional, to portray the conflict between good and evil in the
individual soul:

> Each one begotten by immortal seed,
> Becomes the pitch'd field of two deadly foes,
> Spirit and Flesh: these never are agreed,
> With truceless war each other doth oppose;
> And though the Spirit oft the Flesh doth quell
> It may subdue, but can it not expel,
> So stoutly doth the Jebusite rebel.[8]

The opening stanza presents an interesting Christianized view
of David's punishment and suffering which does, however, emphasize the value of heroic patience:

How Zion's Psalmist grievously offended,
How Israel's Harper did most foully slide,
Yet how that Psalmist penitent amended,
And how that Harper patient did abide
    Deserved chastisement; (so fitly styled,
    Which wrath inflicted not, but love most mild,
    Not for to hurt, but heal a wanton child;)[9]

Fuller's general theme is that trials and suffering are necessary in this life if individuals or nations are to find salvation or peace. God's justice is really God's mercy, for how else could the erring soul be brought to see the truth? Fuller, the moralist, quickly dominated Fuller, the heroic poet, for, although he occasionally adopted a heroic device or attitude, most of the time he relished the opportunity to strike home with a pious application. Even the literal incident of David's writing the command to contrive Uriah's death yields this quaintly conceited moral:

This, certs, I know, as sepian juice did sink
Into his spongy paper, sabling o'er
The same with various-formed specks of ink,
Which was so pure and lily-white before;
    So spots of sin the writer's soul did stain,
    Whose soily tincture did therein remain,
    Till brinish tears had wash'd it out again.[10]

It was important to the theme that Fuller picture David's punishment as following his repentance and as a necessary part of his reconciliation with God. David's anguish at Absalom's treachery he linked with Christ's suffering:

This makes me call my Saviour's grief to mind,
Who on this mount, because the Jews were grown
So wicked,—those that said they saw, so blind—
Mourn'd for their sins, that mourn'd not for their own:
    Much did He weep for others, that forbad
    Others to weep for Him, whose being sad
    Hath made His saints, for ever since, full glad.[11]

The tried and suffering hero is thus clearly a type of Christ, and the elements of temptation, inner conflict, moral choice, with subsequent reward or punishment, are essential aspects of the concept of the Christian hero.

If David represented virtue fallen but redeemed, Joseph was an example of virtue triumphant over temptation. Sylvester's translation of Jerome Fracastor's Latin poem on Joseph (1555) focuses attention upon the major theme in the title, *The Maiden's Blush; or Joseph, Mirror of Modestie, Map of Pietie, Maze of Destinie, Or rather, Divine Providence*. The moral and devotional interest which characterized his translation of the *Judith* is evident in this poem, but there is also a lively interest in the dramatic qualities of the story. The action opens with a brief description of Satan's role in inspiring envy and malice in the hearts of Joseph's brethren, for

> Th' Old Serpent knew (for, much to know is given
> Unto that Hell-god, by the God of Heaven)
> It was decree'd by everlasting Date,
> And promised, that there should propagate,
> From *Abraham's* happy Stock, a holy Stem
> Which should confound th' Infernall Diadem.[12]

Furthermore, the central scene in which Potiphar's wife, Iëmpsar, tempts Joseph to adultery is pictured as being brought to pass by one of Satan's harpies masquerading as Iphicle, the lady's nurse. The innocence of Joseph after the first assay is given a specifically Christian interpretation:

> Faire-featur'd *Joseph,* with his Eyes down bent,
> As inly pitying with a griefe unshown,
> His Ladie's Passions as hee did his own;
> For, hee suppos'd her gaite to Church had bin
> To seek for Mercy and forsake her sin:
> But, nothing lesse; Shee all the gods requires,
> To friend her love, and further her desires;[13]

The neat juxtaposition of the Christian connotations of the Church with the reference to pagan gods serves to emphasize the contrast between true piety and reliance upon false deities. The account of Joseph's fare in prison, "puddle-water, and barly bread,"[14] is perhaps too literal, but Sylvester was more imaginative in proposing that Joseph was sustained by an angelic being who so impressed the jailer that he treated the prisoner with reverence. If Joseph's virtue was assailed by demonic agents, it was reasonable that his fortitude should be rewarded by angelic help.

Fracastor died before he completed the poem, and Sylvester undertook no more than a translation of the existing portion, but Robert Aylett's *Joseph, or Pharaoh's Favorite* (1623) is so often parallel to Sylvester's poem that his completion of the story might serve for both. He adopted the same device of introducing Satan as the source of trouble, but he did so in terms paralleling the Book of Job. Satan is the envious spirit who appears before God with a proposal to test God's chosen favorite, Jacob. God, of course, grants the request, knowing the foreordained outcome; Satan's dispatch of a devil for each of the brothers is but a variation of the procedure:

> He by their malice labours cunningly,
> To ruine *Jacob* and his *Family*
> In *Joseph's* losse: Thus did the envious Fiend
> Project destruction, God a blessed end.[15]

Aylett differed from Sylvester chiefly in his expansion of the classical heroic elements. He introduced, near the beginning, an epic genealogy of the Hebrews down to Joseph, and, when Joseph was brought by the merchants to Egypt, gave an extended account of the history of that country and its accomplishments in learning. From time to time he digressed into specific accounts of the deeds of earlier heroes, Isaac and Jacob,[16] and

inserted an account of the Flood by means of tapestry pictures.[17]
Even the story of Joseph's temptation was related by Joseph
himself late in the poem, and the personal narration allowed
the poet to fit in much commentary on the nature of true love
and chastity.[18] The influence of Du Bartas is evident in the digressions on science, natural history, and travel in the Biblical
lands. Part Du Bartas and part classical is the detailed description of the sun's course through twelve years.[19] There is a curiously middle-class account full of admiration for Joseph's astute
manipulation of Pharaoh's capital,[20] and an equally curious
prophecy of the commercial advantages of cutting a "Suez"
canal.[21] The poem goes much farther toward imitation of classical epic form than Sylvester's, but Aylett was still working primarily in the Renaissance and English tradition with its blend
of narrative interest and devotional purpose. The epitaph which
concludes the poem, however, indicates the qualities which
Aylett considered important in his hero; the implied parallel
with Christ is noteworthy:

> His *Father's* Darling, *mothers* deare delight
> Object of Satan's malice, Brethrens spite
> To Master just; chaste, faithful to his Dame:
> In Prison free, condemn'd, yet void of blame;
> From Dungeon raised to highest reputation,
> By Wisdome, Counsell, Dreames, and Divination;
> Thus God by him a great deliverance wrought,
> In saving them, who his destruction sought:
> A diligent, Wise, provident Observer,
> And therefore of Mankinde a great preserver.[22]

Aylett's use of the Book of Job as a parallel and as a source of
material further suggests the common acceptance of the concept
of a tried and suffering hero. Job was the best human example
of such heroism, and most closely of all the Old Testament
figures typified that aspect of Christ's earthly life.[23] The Book

of Job, however, was in many ways the Old Testament book
farthest removed from the form and spirit of classical heroic
poetry. Although Milton spoke of it as a brief epic, its form was
probably recognized as being closer to drama than to narrative
poetry. Sylvester called his *Job Triumphant in His Triall* a
"Divine and True Tragi-Comedy." Quarles wrote of the subject as a "tragic scene" and a "play" in the proposition to his
Job Militant. The major obstacle to direct heroic treatment was
the fact that the narrative portions provided only a brief outline and framework for the dialogues between Job and his
friends. None of the protagonists other than Job could be
viewed as heroic, nor did they act in any sense beyond the pro-
pounding of various aspects of the problem of suffering. It is
not surprising, therefore, that the three full-length treatments
of Job in the first half of the century are essentially paraphrases.
Sandys simply entitled his poem *A Paraphrase upon Job* and
offered no theological or devotional commentary that might
indicate his interest in the subject. Yet all three undoubtedly
viewed Job as a heroic figure.

Sylvester's paraphrase is the only work which he translated
from the Bible directly. In the proem he indicated that he ap-
proached the translation of the Holy Word with utmost humility, praying, "Let not my sensuall, thy pure Sense defile."[24]
In explaining the purpose of his undertaking, however, he made
a significant comparison between Homer's *Odyssey* and the
Book of Job:

> 'T were labour lost, to fable (Homer-like)
> The strange long Voyage of a wily Greek;
> The Paines, the Perills, and extreme disease
> That hee endured both by Land and Seas;
> Sith sacred *Truth's* Heav'n-prompted Books present
> In *Constant Job* a worthier Argument.[25]

Sylvester's theme is the heroic fortitude required of the faithful
in whom:

> Religious feare of *God* is deep imprest:
> What-ever Stroak of *Fortune* threat his State,
> What-ever Danger him discommodate,
> What-ever Mischiefe that betide him shall,
> What-ever Losse, what-ever Crosse befall:
> Inflexible, invincible pursues
> The sacred Footing he did ever use:
> And ay more constant and confirm'd is Hee,
> The more extreme his sad Afflictions be.[26]

Sylvester's paraphrase is a generally competent piece of work,
though it is characterized by his rather homely diction and his
fondness for compound epithets and extended parentheses. Except in the proem, he refrained from interjecting devotional
material or personal commentary, evidence of his respect for
the profound effectiveness of the Biblical text itself.

Quarles, also, paraphased the text in a direct and literal
manner, but he appended to each chapter a meditation wherein
he elaborated some moral or devotional point in the text in the
manner of a sermon or a catechism. In these meditations,
Quarles often merely paraded "authorities" by drawing moral
or philosophical passages from a wide variety of sources: Horace,
Juvenal, Martial, Seneca, Plato, Aristotle, Boethius, the early
Church Fathers, and the traditional commentaries. These passages are all learnedly glossed in the marginal notes. Although
the Biblical text and the meditations were kept separate, the
total effect is that of a scholarly dissertation on human suffering. To the general theme of patience and fortitude, the meditations added the medieval theme of contempt for the world
with its emphasis upon decay and corruption, worms and dust.
Quarles, however, was no advocate of mere resignation or re-
tirement from the world. He constantly reiterated the need for

individual struggle and perseverance in such morsels as these:

> Thy life's a Warfare, Thou a Souldier art,
> Satan's thy Foe-man, and a faithfull Heart,
> Thy two-edg'd Weapon, Patience thy Shield,
> Heaven is thy Chiefetain, and the world thy Field.
>
> . . . .
>
> Our Life's a Road, in death our Iourney ends;
> We goe on God's Embassage; some, he sends
> Gall'd with the trotting of hard Misery,
> And others, pacing on Prosperity:
> Some lagge, whilest others gallop on, before;
> All goe an end, some faster, and some slower.[27]

Quarles's conclusion in "The Digestion of the Whole Historie" is that "Affliction is a Rod, to scourge us Home,/ A painfull Earnest of a Heaven to come."[28]

Apparently, Quarles saw Job primarily as an example of the warfare between good and evil in the world as it affects man, who shares the fruits of original sin but who can, through the imputed righteousness made possible by Christ, ensure his salvation by faith and fortitude. The heroism of Job was thus directly related to the life of each individual through the common experience of trial and suffering. It was a concept of Christian heroism which Spenser and Bunyan could portray vividly in allegorical form, but it was not easily portrayed in classical epic form. Quarles's careful separation of the narrative and the devotional material indicates the parting of the ways to which the religious poet with a devotional purpose but an admiration for classical form eventually came. Quarles was unable to choose and set out on both ways at once. The method he adopted was wholly familiar, for he simply fell back upon the pulpit technique of presenting the text and expounding the application. The heroic note was there, but it was drowned out by the sonorous tones of the preacher.

In his *Historie of Samson* (1631) Quarles felt surer of the heroic nature of the subject and allowed himself greater freedom in expanding and embellishing the text. What is most noteworthy is the semidramatic device of long conversations and soliloquies which Quarles employed to fill out the bare narrative outline. The poet was not interested in description or stirring accounts of Samson's great deeds, but in the three main trials of the hero at the hands of women. The first trial was his bride's begging for the secret of the Lion and Honey riddle and her betrayal of the secret to the Philistines. Samson's revenge on this occasion, however, was a trespass against God's will and against his vows as a Nazarite. The second trial was of his lust for the harlot, which Quarles used to enforce the moral that, though the weakness of the flesh must be paid for in tears, such trials teach the soul:

> If man were perfect, and entirely good,
> He were not man: He were not flesh and blood:
> Or should he never fall, he would, at length,
> Not see his weaknesse, and presume in strength:[29]

Samson thus became also an example of the danger of presumption and overconfidence; Quarles stressed the fact that as a consequence of this sin Samson was humbled and knew real fear. The third trial was Delilah's winning of the secret of his strength, and again it was lust and overconfidence which the poet saw as the causes of Samson's downfall. Samson's restoration to the role of hero took place only after he had sincerely repented his presumption and self-reliance, and acknowledged himself to be the humble instrument of God. His death, Quarles indicated, was a heroic and glorious one:

> Thus died our *Samson,* whose brave death has won
> More honour, then his honour's life had done:
> Thus died our *Conquerour*; whose latest breath
> Was crown'd with Conquest; triumph'd over death;

> Thus died our *Samson*; whose last drop of blood
> Redeem'd heaven's glory, and his Kingdome's good
> Thus dy'd heaven's *Champion,* and earth's bright *Glory*:[30]

The significance of suffering and repentance is the chief concern of Quarles's *A Feast for Wormes . . . the History of Jonah* and Zachary Boyd's *Historie of Jonah*. In his proposition, Quarles adopted the heroic manner:

> 'T is not the Record of Great *Hector's* Glory,
> Whose matchlesse Valour makes the World a Story.
>
> . . . .
>
> I sing the Praises of Great Judah's Lyon,
> The fragrant Flowre of Jesse, the Lambe of Sion;
>
> . . . .
>
> He acting GOD and MAN in double Nature,
> Did reconcile Mankind, and Man's Creator.[31]

The interest is not, however, in Jonah as a hero, but in the whole story as a demonstration of God's mercy when man repents. Like Samson, Jonah must realize that he is an instrument of God; but unlike Samson, who is an instrument of vengeance, Jonah must be taught that compassion also is an attribute of God. The theme emphasizes the New Testament concept of God as pitying man, and hence places greater stress upon the role of Christ. Prayer and repentance in the Christian hero's relationship with God were linked, through the hope for mercy, with trial and suffering as an instructive discipline to be accepted with patience and fortitude.

Quarles's treatment of the Old Testament figures as representing various aspects of the Christian character provides no clear-cut concept of heroism that can be portrayed in a single individual. Like Spenser, who isolated and abstracted the vices and virtues, Quarles found in each of the Old Testament figures certain distinct examples of Christian heroism. Like Spenser's heroes, whose particular virtues would have been summed up, eventually, in the magnanimity of Prince Arthur, the Old Testament figures all typified aspects of the supreme virtue represented by Christ. Quarles was primarily a devotional poet whose interest in heroic poetry led him to attempt moral histories in narrative form. His efforts resulted in little more than expanded and embellished paraphrases of the Biblical text. He adopted the heroic manner, usually in the proposition and invocation, but otherwise made no consistent attempt to imitate the classical form. He told the stories in chronological fashion as they happened; he introduced no narrative digressions or episodes, used extended similes sparingly, and apparently had no interest in supernatural machinery not already indicated in the Biblical text. Yet he talked continually of heroism, with many side glances at the classical heroes. In the last analysis, he was unable to compromise his moral and devotional concern with the prevailing concept of heroic poetry. His true bent lay in the direction of subjective piety and didacticism, not in the direction of objective narrative portrayal of morality.

Cowley's *Davideis,* the last of the works to be considered in this chapter, was in many respects the antithesis of Quarles's narrative poems. Cowley had no overwhelming passion for pious devotions such as ruled Quarles, but he did have intense admiration for the classics, in particular Virgil. Even his definite statement of commitment to sacred subjects in the preface (1656) was subsequently shown to be a temporary enthusiasm by his return to secular and profane subjects. It is reasonable to suppose that the young Cowley, growing up at a time when Biblical narrative poetry was extremely popular and widely written, with such major examples as Sylvester's translation of Du Bartas and Quarles's poems at hand, should see in the Bible the best source of material for an epic comparable to Virgil's. With Cowley the medieval heritage of traditional devotional and didactic forms was no longer a strong influence, and his academic training in the classics at Cambridge permanently fixed his preference for classical forms. In the *Davideis* Cowley sought to combine the two main interests which operated in heroic narrative poetry in the first half of the century: the enthusiasm for Biblical, and in particular Old Testament, subjects, and the admiration for the classical epic form and spirit. The difference between Cowley and his predecessors in Biblical narrative poetry was that Cowley, as he said in his preface, set out to write a Christian epic in classical form and then decided that the Bible offered ideal matter, not because he was ardently religious but because he thought he saw new possibilities of an artistic order.

There is no need to burden this study with a critical analysis of the work as a whole. What is of main concern in this discussion is the way in which Cowley attempted to handle the problem of making David a hero in keeping with the classical spirit and form of the work. J. M. McBryde long ago began the practice of pointing out the parallels between incidents or episodes in the *Davideis* and those in Virgil and other writers up to Crashaw.[32] Cowley's concept of the Christian hero in relation to the heroism portrayed in the English Biblical narratives has not, however, been considered.

The figure of David could exemplify many different moral aspects, but the most popular theme had been the fall, repentance, and punishment of David for his adultery with Bathsheba. David in this respect illustrated the Christian concern with trial and suffering, the justice of God's retribution, and the mercy granted after heartfelt repentance. Cowley, however, showed little interest in these aspects of the Christian hero. Patience and faith in God were undoubtedly important elements in his conception, but he was interested also in the classical heroic qualities of loyalty, courage, and martial prowess. In

this sense he was closer to the conception which Drayton had
begun to develop in the fragment on *David and Golia*. In the
preface (1656) Cowley explained his choice of David:

For what worthier subject could have been chosen among all the
Treasuries of past times then the life of this young Prince, who from
so small beginnings, through such infinite troubles and oppositions,
by such miraculous virtues and excellencies, and with such incompa-
rable variety of wonderful actions and accidents, became the greatest
Monarch that ever sat upon the most famous Throne of the whole
Earth? whom should a Poet more justly seek to honour then the
highest person who ever honored his Profession? whom a Christian
Poet rather then the man after Gods own heart, and the man who
had that sacred pre-eminence above all other Princes, to be the best
and mightiest of that Royal Race from whence *Christ* himself according to the flesh disdained not to descend?[33]

Taken together with other parts of the preface which outline his plan for the structure of the epic, this passage strongly
indicates that Cowley was not interested in David merely as
a moral example of the Quarles's kind. He speaks of the variety
of wonderful actions which the whole reign of David provided,
and proposes to "interweave upon several occasions ... most of
the illustrious Stories of the Old Testament."[34] David became
the center of a richly significant period of history and culture
encompassing not only his own actions but also those which
foreshadowed the coming of Christ. Cowley thus moved away
from the limited scope of the individual "history" toward a
design which had a wider range of epic action. In a sense it was
a move back to the larger Christian view of universal history
which Du Bartas had begun to develop in the *Second Weeke*.
Cowley's design was to present the Old Testament material by
means of epic episodes and digressions in a unified classical
structure rather than chronologically as in Du Bartas's work. The
cosmic range of action with Christ as the culmination was unquestionably what Cowley intended to show in classical epic

form—something that had not been done before. It is important not only that he began the life of David *in medias res,* but
also that he portrayed David as a kind of midpoint in the Old
Testament history between Creation and Christ; so the cosmic
action also, as it were, begins *in medias res.*

The four completed books contain an amazing amount of
evidence that Cowley continually had the cosmic action in
mind. The invocation is addressed directly to Christ as the Redeemer of the world. Not only did he make use of the hexameral theme of Satan's enmity working upon Saul, but also,
at the end of the first book, he introduced a description of Creation as part of his digression on the Prophets' College at Ramah.[35]
In the second book there is a digression on the story of Abraham as represented on a tapestry,[36] but even more significant is
the vision of David when the angel Gabriel prophesies the succession of David's line down to Christ.[37] In the third book the
story of Lot is presented in the form of a picture, for Lot was
the father of the Moabites with whom David took refuge in his
flight from Saul. The story of David's life from his birth to his
escape from Saul is told in a narrative episode by Joab for the
entertainment of the Moabites. In the fourth book the history
of Saul down to the time of his rash vow to sacrifice Jonathan
is related by David himself, who also provides an epic genealogy
of the Hebrew people. In this book Saul really becomes the central moral example; and, as Samuel Johnson pointed out, Cowley "gives Saul both the body and mind of a hero."[38] Significantly, it is David who tells the story and who hopes, despite
Samuel's prophecy of Saul's doom, that Saul will repent and be
restored to grace.

Cowley had already managed in the first four books alone to
cover a surprising range and variety of material. But there remained an enormous amount still to be covered, even if he
brought the immediate action only to the death of Saul and

Jonathan. The scope of the epic action set up in these first books is unmistakably that of universal history; even though restriced to the Old Testament history between Creation and Christ, the range of material is staggering to contemplate, as it would have accumulated through eight more books. The difference between Cowley's plan and Milton's accomplished epic design becomes all the more apparent when one realizes that they were dealing with essentially the same scope of action. By centering the action on David, Cowley condemned himself to innumerable digressions and episodes to fill out the cosmic drama. Milton, by centering the action on the original Fall within the cosmic setting, greatly simplified this aspect of the problem.

In other respects, however, Cowley's plan was close to that of the classical epic, and particularly that of Virgil. David, like Aeneas, is a man of destiny whose own fortunes are part of a larger action. He is noble, courageous, glorious in battle, involved in an unhappy episode with a woman, but strong enough to bear the trials and vicissitudes of fortune. As a type of Christian hero, he is preëminently the man of God, with strong faith, capable of recognizing his sin and sincerely repenting his fall, and patient in bearing the punishment which God justly visits upon him. The combination of classical and Christian qualities of heroism apparently caused Cowley no concern, and it must be admitted that of all the Old Testament heroes David, in both the active and the contemplative sense, best suited such a combination. The opening proposition of the work is a convincing one:

> I sing the Man who Judah's Scepter bore,
> In that right Hand which held the Crook before;
> Who from best Poet, best of Kings did grow;
> The two chief Gifts Heav'n could on Man bestow.
> Much Danger first, much Toil did he sustain,
> Whilst Saul and Hell crost his strong Fate in vain.
> Nor did his Crown less painful Work afford,

Less exercise his Patience, or his Sword;
So long her Conqu'ror Fortune's spight pursued;
Till with unwearied Virtue he subdu'd
All homebred Malice, and all foreign Boasts;
Their Strength was Armies, his the Lord of Hosts.[39]

The elements of Christian heroism, patience, faith, virtue, trial and suffering, repentance and forgiveness, brought out by Cowley's predecessors in the Biblical narrative are all present in David. The ultimate meaning of these qualities lies in the central fact of Christ as the climax of universal history and the institution of a Christian morality. Cowley unquestionably undertook to establish the universal setting of the action in the first two books, drawing upon all the rich cosmic association of the hexameral themes and providing a vision of the coming of Christ. Yet, apparently, the structural importance of this setting has not been recognized, and the work has been criticized mainly because it seems to lack the immediate unity and coherence of Virgil's epic.[40] The initial impresison is certainly one of diffuseness and undigested variety, and it may very well be true that Cowley would have failed to bring all to order. Yet, when the work is viewed in terms of the experiments with Biblical materials and themes from Du Bartas onward in the first half of the century, the impression grows that Cowley was consciously building upon concepts which had already been developed and which he assumed his readers would recognize. In this sense, he is truly in direct line with Milton, projecting in a full-scale classical epic design the wealth of Christian associations to be found in a Biblical subject and portraying a pattern of Christian heroism in a human protagonist, acting and suffering and triumphing in the cosmic setting of universal history.

CHAPTER IV

NEW TESTAMENT NARRATIVES

THE proportion of narratives and heroic poems based on New Testament materials is surprisingly small in view of the dominant interest in a Christian epic or heroic poetry. Yet the Atonement made by Christ was always regarded as the central act in the drama of world history, and the Redemption the most important event for the life of the individual Christian. The greater popularity of hexameral and Old Testament subjects for narrative and heroic poetry does not mean that the New Testament was less important in the religious thought of the period. On the contrary, the devotional poetry produced so abundantly at this time was almost wholly concerned with the meaning of Christ for the world and the souls of men. But narrative treatments of the life of Christ or of events related to Christ were, apparently, another matter.

The Middle Ages had produced some narrative and dramatic poetry dealing with the life of Christ as a historical event, but the traditional emphasis was upon its spiritual significance. Even in such a vigorous poem as the Old English *Christ and Satan,* the emphasis was primarily upon the rewards and punishments of the life hereafter, and the broken and defeated figure of Satan was meant to provide a stern warning to resist temptation. The stanzaic *Life of Christ* (fourteenth century) and the *Cursor Mundi* both treated Christ in the framework of universal history and thus stressed the climactic role of Christ rather than the individual events of his human life. Perhaps the most direct and dramatic portrayals of Christ were in the mystery plays, but these too were centered upon theologically significant events such as the Birth, the Flight into Egypt, the Temptation, the Passion, and the Resurrection. For the poets of the first half of the seventeenth century, Christ remained the climactic figure in universal history and the center of devotional life. He was the Hero of the cosmic drama and the ultimate model of Christian heroism for his followers. Protestantism tended to teach that Christ was not only the means of Atonement and Redemption but also a manifestation of human potential which could be aspired to through faith. The medieval Church had expressed much the same idea in the elaborate lives of the saints and martyrs, but the Protestants rejected the apparatus of the saints and the theory of mediation, and turned rather to the power of Christ manifested in the life of the individual Christian. Joseph Fletcher described the pattern of individual redemption in this way:

> And though God's image in which Man was made,
> By sin's approach was totally decaid;
> But he could then, nor doe, nor think aright,
> All was so faulty in his Maker's sight.
> Yet is't by grace in Christ so well refin'd,
> That God with man-renu'd, no fault will finde,
> For MAN thereby is all so purifi'd,
> As that he can God's fiery triall bide.[1]

Such, also, was Bunyan's vision of the heroism of the wayfaring Christian.

A basic distinction must be made between the figural or symbolic significance of Christ as the center of the cosmic drama and the human significance of Christ as the supreme example of heroism for the individual soul. The problem of treating Christ in a narrative poem lay in the difficulty posed by the paradox of the divine and the human coexisting in one nature. The profound mystery of the Incarnation and the Atonement, central in all Christian thought, dominated and overshadowed the human events of the life of Christ. Although the Birth, the

---

[1] For notes to chapter iv see page 145.

Temptation in the Wilderness, and the Passion had traditionally been presented as emphasizing the human aspects of trial and suffering necessary for Redemption, the Atonement itself was inconceivable as anything but a Divine Act. The figure of Christ was thus primarily an ambiguous one, a combination of divine and human, or a manifestation of the divine in the human. It was difficult to separate the two aspects and almost impossible to treat wholly of one or the other.

In the Christian tradition, both aspects had been presented. The divine and celestial nature of Christ received emphasis in such themes as the Harrowing of Hell, in which the cosmic struggle between good and evil ended in the triumph of the Divine Principle. Christ in these terms was the Conqueror and Victor, a heroic figure of immeasurable proportions, transcending any concept of human heroism. In the earthly realm, the miracles of Christ were treated as evidence of the divine nature. Miracles were obviously not events of human origin nor, indeed, susceptible of explanation by the limited human reason. Yet the human trial and suffering of Christ were also of major importance, for it was essential to the concept of the Atonement that the consequences of the first human Fall in Adam be paid for in the human Passion of the Second Adam. Whereas the Atonement was a satisfaction of Divine Justice, the Redemption was an act of Divine Mercy with results manifest in the human rather than the celestial realm. Christ as the Redeemer was thus a more human figure than Christ the Conqueror. The medieval stress upon the sacrifice as payment in human terms for human sin led eventually to the emphasis upon the terrible suffering of the Passion. Vida, in his *Christiad,* stated unequivocally that Christ, in the final hour on the Cross, suffered wholly in his human nature:

> For 'midst the terrors of this trying hour,
>   Divested, as it were, of heav'nly power,
> Helpless, unarm'd, and mortal he is found.[2]

Nowhere else is the dual nature of Christ more clearly manifested than in the Passion and death. Christ represented man,
but his suffering and death were ordained by God. Christian
theologians had stated the essential paradox in many ways, but
among the early Church Fathers, Irenaeus had given one of
the most straightforward expressions of the inherent duality:

If man had not defeated the enemy of man, the enemy would not
have been fairly [*juste*] overcome. Again, if God had not bestowed
salvation, we should not possess it securely. And if man had not been
united with God, he would not have been able to become partaker
of immortality. For the mediator between God and man must through
His relation to both bring both together into friendship and concord,
that He might both present man to God, and that man might learn
to know God.[3]

There was thus another way in which Christ was especially
meaningful for his human followers: through his human example and ministry "man might learn to know God." The imitation of Christ had long been of major importance in Church
teaching, and, as imitation could be only in human terms, it
was natural that emphasis should fall on the earthly life of
Christ. Imitation, however, required not only understanding
the spiritual significance of Christ but also the undergoing of
trial and suffering in the spirit of Christ where necessary. The
saints and martyrs were the most dramatic human examples of
such imitation, but in the life of the average Christian, also, the
virtues of humility, obedience to the Will of God, incessant
struggle against temptation, and patience in tribulation were
proofs of spiritual strength. Such was the essentially human application of the doctrine set forth by Paul in the Epistle to the
Romans 12:1—"I beseech you therefore, brethren, by the mercies of God, that ye present your bodies a living sacrifice, holy,
acceptable unto God, which is your reasonable service." The
preparation of the individual soul for salvation involved sacri-

fice and suffering, and such trial was not only imitation of
Christ's example but also symbolically an act of atonement
within human capacities. Christ the Teacher and Example thus
had the most immediate significance for the human soul strug-
gling through temptations to the salvation made possible by
Christ the Redeemer.

The figure of Christ was not easily reducible within the scope
of a single view or readily manageable in human terms as the
protagonist of a narrative poem. There were three aspects of
Christ which could be emphasized, but eventually the three
were inseparable. Christ as Victor or Conqueror belonged obviously to the hexameral theme of the cosmic drama; in the
conflict between good and evil, between Christ and Satan, the
setting was all of Creation, and the prize was Man. The action
was wholly supernatural and, although immeasurably important for mankind, took place outside the area of purely human
struggle. Christ as Redeemer operated more fully within the
human realm, for the sacrifice and suffering necessary for the
Atonement had to be in human terms. Within the scope of
universal history, and especially in the Christian interpretation
of the history set forth in the Old Testament, the emphasis fell
upon Christ as Redeemer. The human stories and personages
of the Old Testament were meaningful primarily because they
prefigured the elements essential to Redemption.

Finally, Christ as Example, the figure presented in the Gospels, provided the most immediate model for action in the
human and earthly struggle with evil. For the Protestant the
major concern was the conflict which was carried on unceas-
ingly in the human soul. The themes of spiritual pilgrimage
and warfare, medieval and traditional though they were, became far more specific and concrete, more everyday and real,
in the seventeenth-century Protestant concepts, than they had
been in the older morality plays. For Bunyan, the Christian life,

as portrayed in *The Pilgrim's Progress,* is one of trial and tribulation; the Christian hero can persevere only by virtue of his faith in Redemption, and is guided, in his search for salvation, only by a somewhat unreliable conscience and by the teachings and example of Christ in the Bible. The action takes place primarily in the human and earthly realm rather than the cosmic, although there are hexameral elements in the battle with Apollyon, and the Celestial City fittingly symbolizes salvation after death.

It is nevertheless apparent that as subject for narrative poetry, the three aspects of Christ could never be completely separated. No matter how much emphasis was placed upon the human aspects, the significance of the human ultimately lay in the cosmic action. If the cosmic drama was stressed, the consequences were eventually meaningful only as they were manifest in human affairs. Christ was truly the mediator between divine and human, between cosmic and earthly; the essential paradox could never be solved by merely shifting the emphasis or restricting the vision, for the human spirit can be satisfied by a paradox that remains an ineffable mystery, but the human reason balks at a mystery that seems only a distorted paradox. The narrative poets who used Biblical subject matter in the first half of the seventeenth century would settle for nothing less than the whole mystery, or, as they saw it, the miracle of God's mercy and goodness. It was inevitable, then, that the paradox of Christ should be central in all their concerns, whether they used hexameral, Old Testament, or New Testament subjects. Christ was the ultimate Hero, or measure of heroism, yet as a subject for heroic poetry the figure of Christ was too complex, too paradoxical, to be encompassed in a single or restricted vision whether it be cosmic or human.[4]

In view of the difficulties inherent in any attempt to treat the life of Christ directly and literally in heroic narrative form, it is not surprising that most of the narrative poets should have had recourse to allegorical forms. A reason is not hard to find when one perceives that the central theme of these works is the conflict between good and evil. The question is whether the setting of the conflict is cosmic or human. If the setting is cosmic, the need for allegory is minimal, for the conflict is between Christ and Satan, both historical figures. If the setting is human, the need for allegory is greatly increased, because the concepts of good and evil in human experience are primarily abstractions when viewed as motives for action. The consequences of good or evil can be portrayed in realistic terms, but good or evil motives had long been dramatically portrayed as personified abstractions. The medieval and Spenserian tradition of allegory was too strong and too dramatically effective to be ignored by the Biblical narrative poets. If some sort of bridge between the cosmic and the human was made necessary by the subject, allegory provided the most readily workable connection, holding together as it did the abstract and the concrete, the spirit and the body, the supernatural and the natural.

The distinction must be kept, however, between incidental allegory and the allegorical form of narrative. A special kind of incidental allegory is that found in association with the machinations of Satan and the infernal council. For most Christian readers at this time the enmity of Satan and the fiendish horde was more actual than figurative, yet as dramatic embodiments of evil the devils belong in the same category as all other personified powers of good and evil. It is not surprising that the traditional personifications of the deadly sins and other vices—Envy, Lust, Pride, Cruelty, Wrath, and so forth—should become associated with the devils as the means by which Satan hoped to win his ends. Two sources contributed to the portrayal of these allegorical figures: one was the traditional extended description, most clearly developed in the induction to the *Mirror for Magistrates*; the other was the classical device of the Fury such as Alecto in Book VII of the *Aeneid,* the agent of grief and discord. In the descriptions of Hell both elements usually appear: the detailed portrayal of the vices in their dens and caves, and the calling forth of one of the Furies for a special evil purpose. In Beaumont's *Psyche* there are three different descriptions of the regions of Hell on the three occasions when Satan calls up a particular Fury: Lust in Canto I, Jealousy in Canto VIII, and Avarice in Canto XI. Satan also employs the hag Famine in Canto IX, Calumny in Canto XIII, and Heresy in Canto XVIII. Milton's description of Sin and Death in Book II of *Paradise Lost,* although it has Biblical warranty in James 1:15, seems to be related to this tradition if not actually part of it. Allegorical narrative, in contrast, was usually adopted as the dominant form in works whose primary theme was the pilgrimage of the soul or the warfare between good and evil for possession of the soul.

Because there are relatively few English works on New Testament subjects, it would be profitable to look briefly at Vida's *Christiad* as an example of what had been done in sixteenth-century Italy with a heroic treatment of the life of Christ. It provides a more elaborate illustration than any English work before Cowley and Milton of the careful joining of traditional Christian materials and classical epic form. Vida, as a Catholic bishop, was concerned principally with the orthodoxy of his material, but he was also in the main stream of Italian neo-classicism and interested in achieving the dignity proper to his form.

Vida's epic is essentially a highly elaborated Passion, for he selected as the main action of the poem the last days of Christ from his entry into Jerusalem to the Resurrection and final appearances to the disciples. Episodic narratives and digressions, however, fill out the work until the total picture of the cosmic drama from Creation to Doomsday is complete. All aspects of Christ—Conqueror, Redeemer, and Example—are represented as the action ranges from the cosmic to the minutely human. The conflict between good and evil is portrayed not only in the cosmic setting by means of the machinations of Satan, but also in the human realm in the temptations of the disciples, of the Jewish leaders, of Pilate, and in particular of Judas. In addition, nearly all the major Old Testament figures are cited as figurative examples. Not only is the hexameral set piece of the infernal council and Satan's employment of various Furies fully developed, but the story of the Battle in Heaven and the fall of Satan's host is also brought in as part of the symbolism of Christ's triumph in death. Throughout the work, Vida continually used the term "Hero" (*pulcherrimus heros*) for Christ, and even in the elaborate description of the humiliation of the Cross, he maintained the sublime and dignified tone.

A brief survey of the structure of the work reveals both the range of the subject matter and the rigid classical form. Book I opens with a proposition and invocation in the classical style and launches immediately into the description of Christ's last journey to Jerusalem. To the exultant disciples who see their entry into Jerusalem as a triumphal procession of the Messiah, Christ prophesies the true nature of coming events:

> I go, and chearfully my Death embrace,
> To screen from Vengeance Man's devoted race.
> This is the weighty burden, these the woes,
> Thou, father Adam! did'st on Me impose;
> Thyself the tempting fruit did'st bear away,
> And I the dreadful Forfeiture must pay.
> But the third orient Moon, th' Atonement made,
> I'll rise triumphant from the gloomy shade.[5]

This statement of the cosmic drama is followed by a change of scene to Hell, where Satan addresses the infernal council. In

Jerusalem, Christ works many miracles, and then in the Temple explains the significance of the Fall by means of paintings of the Creation which adorn the dome. Noah, Abraham, Joseph, and Moses are also brought in as figures of Christ. In solitary meditation and prayer on the Mount, Christ holds communion with God, and Vida presents God as speaking directly in answer. The book closes with Christ wrapped in glory.

In Book II the demons attempt to subvert the disciples, but Satan himself undertakes the assault of Judas. The Last Supper and the betrayal of Christ in the Garden of Gethsemane are the major incidents, but, while describing the Senate of the Jewish priests and their deliberations, Vida digresses in a long catalogue of the tribes of Israel and Judah and the annual assembly of the tribes for the Passover. During the Last Supper the disciples are regaled with the heroic story of Moses and the crossing of the Red Sea.

In Book III Joseph and John go to intercede for Christ with Pilate; Joseph first recounts the genealogy of Israel and Judah from Abraham down to Mary, then tells the story of Mary's Visitation, his own role as appointed husband, the birth of Christ at Bethlehem, and the Flight into Egypt. Christ's childhood and early miracles conclude the book. In Book IV John takes up the story, again emphasizes the cosmic background of the Creation and Fall, and tells of John the Baptist as the last of the prophets of Christ. Most of John's narrative is concerned with interpretation of Christ's ministry and miracles, with devotional stress upon the essence of Christ's teachings, the principles of love and mercy, and the rejection of worldly glory, wealth, and fame. Vida gives a very short account of the Temptation in the Wilderness, treating it as one of the many miraculous incidents in the life of Christ rather than as a human conflict.

Book V comes back to the main action with dramatic scenes of the trial, the torment, and the Crucifixion. Pilate attempts to save Christ, but Satan calls up the Furies, Fear and Sloth, to undermine him, and Pilate gives way before the angry crowd that threatens insurrection. Vida dwells upon the Crucifixion itself with all the horrifying realism possible. It is a terrifyingly detailed description of Christ's agony, and Vida makes clear that in the final hour Christ's suffering was wholly human. After Christ's death, the scene at once moves to Heaven and pictures the angry hosts of angelic beings forming in battle array for swift and awful vengeance. God speaks in thunder to restrain the angelic hosts, giving an affirmation of Supreme Power reminiscent of the speech in the Book of Job and an exposition of the Divine Plan for Atonement and Redemption.

The concluding book presents a vivid description of the Harrowing of Hell and Christ's leading forth of the righteous souls. The Resurrection is presented primarily as it affected the sorrowing Marys and the fearful priests. Christ's appearances to the apostles are reported and explained by the apostles themselves as they prepare to take up the burden of ministry laid upon them. There is a prophecy of the Second Coming and of the Day of Judgment. The scene in Heaven at Christ's Ascension is full of sublime poetry, much of it drawn from the Psalms, and again Vida presents God as speaking and explaining the significance of the whole cosmic drama. The book concludes with a rapid survey of the work of the apostles, the spread of Christianity through the world, and, of course, the affirmation of the Church of Rome as the means of preserving the apostolic succession.

It can be seen from this brief description how very similar in structure are the *Christiad* and Cowley's *Davideis*. Both limit the scope of the main action, but both fill out the universal background until the whole sweep of the cosmic drama is figured in the immediate events. Satan and the demons are more than supernatural machinery of a classical sort, though the parallel with the gods in Homer and Virgil is a convenient one. They are an essential part of the contest between good and evil, part of the vast design in which Satan continues the struggle with God, even though he knows the foreordained end, for it is through the trials and suffering occasioned by evil that man comes to understand the real meaning of God and salvation. Vida has Satan address the infernal council in almost despairing terms as the last contest between Christ and Satan approaches:

> Yet Him, tho' cloath'd in Human Nature frail
> Our arms and malice but in vain assail.
> With guileful arts the Youth I oft pursu'd,
> Th' attack, tho' vanquish'd, still as oft renew'd;
> (Not by a foolish Ignorance betray'd,
> Th' event was certain e'er the Plots were laid)
> Vary'd my shape, and ev'ry measure press'd,
> To win admittance to his cautious breast.
> In vain; each art undaunted he defy'd;
> Nor on the aid of Arms or Force rely'd;
> With chosen maxims drawn from books of old,
> My wiles he baffled, and my rage controul'd.[6]

Cowley presented Satan in the infernal council plotting David's downfall as part of the same universal struggle:

> And well he knew what Legacy did place,
> The sacred Scepter in blest Judah's Race,
> From which th' Eternal Shilo was to spring;
> A Knowledge which new Hells to Hell did bring!
> And though no less he knew himself too weak
> The smallest Link of strong-wrought Fate to break;
> Yet would he rage, and struggle with the Chain;
> Lov'd to *rebel*, though sure that 'twas *in vain*.[7]

When we turn from the *Christiad* or the *Davideis* to *Paradise Lost*, we realize at once how closely Milton was working within the Christian epic tradition and that the major materials of his design were already available. Milton's Satan is a far more

dramatic and important figure than Vida's or Cowley's, but that
is because Milton chose to emphasize the drama of the conflict
between good and evil in its cosmic setting. Satan's role as the
Antagonist is traditional, but Milton saw that the conflict in
the cosmic setting had a terrible majesty. In Milton's design,
the hexameral set piece of Satan and the infernal council is
brought into full perspective as an essential element, not as a
convenient piece of epic machinery. It is clear, also, that in the
great conflict, Christ is the Protagonist, the Hero, who from the
beginning undertakes the vanquishing of Satan. The Son, in
Milton's design, is not only the Creator but also the Victor who
hurls Satan and the rebellious angels down to Hell. And it is
the Son who becomes the Advocate for fallen man and who
undertakes the heavy task of Atonement and Redemption. Because Milton's concern for the human aspects of the conflict
was also great, he chose as his central action the Temptation
and the Fall in which he could portray the essential humanity
of Adam and Eve. Vida had made the human life of Christ the
center of his main action, and Cowley had chosen a portion of
David's life for his, but the total design is the same in all three.
The central action of each takes place in an earthly setting, but
is meaningful only as it reflects or focuses the larger struggle.
The differences in the three works, therefore, are primarily
those of emphasis and proportion in the design of the materials.
Milton's genius in portraying the drama of the conflict is another
question, perhaps; yet it is impossible to conceive of his success
without considering the effectiveness of his epic design.

Giles Fletcher's *Christ's Victorie* is the first English work in
this period to center the action upon Christ as Hero. It was an
ambitious undertaking by a youth who aspired to leap straight
into the writing of heroic poetry without the conventional
period of trial and preparation in the pastoral and other lesser
genres. In one sense it was too ambitious a project, as Fletcher

himself realized, for at the end of the poem he recognized the greater propriety of his brother Phineas' work in the pastoral. Yet it is significant that he should choose for his first major subject the highest and noblest aspects of the Christian matter. His Christ is primarily Christ as Conqueror in the cosmic drama, and his interest in the human aspects of the action is extremely limited. Although he achieved a certain unity in restricting the action to the four main events of theological importance in the life of Christ—the Birth, the Temptation, the Passion, and the Resurrection—he did not develop the action in essentially epic terms. The two main influences were Spenser and Du Bartas in about equal proportions: the action presented in allegorical form and the theme elaborated in the devotional discursive form. Fletcher conceived the conflict between good and evil as abstract and symbolic, and adopted, in the second book in particular, the Spenserian allegory of temptation. The concrete details he desired to picture are not so much those of individual experience as those of a general, symbolic nature.

A brief outline of the work will clarify the elements that are of interest to this study. The first book has little action of narrative interest; it is primarily a debate in Heaven between Justice and Mercy regarding the significance of the Incarnation and the coming Atonement. The poet describes both allegorical personages in detail in the manner of Spenser's portrait of Nature in the Mutability Cantos or in the style of the medieval portraits of Fortune. It is natural that a debate between Justice and Mercy on this question would be primarily theological in import, and, since the outcome is clear to begin with, there is no real sense of drama. What Fletcher does achieve by this allegorical device, however, is a strong sense of the cosmic implications of the divine action. Justice argues that God should fling away "the world's rude dunghill," "the drosse of the olde chaos," and let man, captive like Satan, spend his weary life in sin and pride.

Mercy, however, points to the allegorical figures of Repentance and Faith as sufficient cause for consideration of man's redemption. Fletcher is fascinated by the violent contrasts of the divine-human paradox, as seen in this stanza from Mercy's speech:

> A Child He was, and had not learn't to speake,
> That with His word the world before did make;
> His mother's armes Him bore, He was so weake,
> That with one hand the vaults of Heau'n could shake;
> See how small roome my infant Lord doth take,
>   Whom all the world is not enough to hold!
>   Who of His yeares, or of His age hath told?
> Neuer such age so young, neuer a child so old.°

Yet these are elements more appropriate to devotional poetry than to a heroic poem; in the first book, Christ is referred to and commented upon, but is not present as an active agent.

In the second book, the Temptation, Fletcher begins to move closer to direct narrative form in the opening stanzas but, after a description of Christ modeled closely upon the Song of Solomon, reverts to allegory. Satan appears in the Spenserian guise of a pious aged hermit, but Fletcher does not present the temptations in direct form. Instead, Satan leads Christ to the House of Despair and to the pavilion of Presumption. The allegory is clear enough: Despair tempts Christ to perform a miracle and to satisfy his hunger by turning stone into bread; Presumption tempts Christ with the vanities and glories of the world. It is Presumption who dares Christ to throw himself from a pinnacle to prove his divinity, but she herself falls headlong. The transition to the garden of Vaine-Glory is a sudden one after the fall of Presumption, but in the garden, a veritable Bower of Bliss, Fletcher expands the allegory in the personifications of Luxury, Ambition, Lust, and Avarice. In this respect, Fletcher moves away from the specific temptations set forth in the Gospels, into a far more Spenserian world.

In the third book, Fletcher almost entirely abandons the
Spenserian allegorical form and turns toward the combination
of narrative and devotion which Du Bartas had developed.
Christ is hardly more prominent as an active agent, but the
setting is not allegorical except for the introduction of the hexameral theme of Satan and the demons as the supernatural
inspirers of Christ's trial and death. Fletcher's Satan addressing
the infernal council has little of the grandeur of Milton's conception:

> See how the world smiles in eternall peace;
> While we, the harmles brats and rustie throng
> Of night, our snakes in curles doe pranke and dresse:
> Why sleep our drouzie scorpions so long?
> Whear is our wonted vertue to doe wrong?
>   Are we our selues? or are we Graces growen?
>   The sonnes of hell or heau'n? was neuer knowne
> Our whips so ouer-moss't and brands so deadly blowne![10]

Significantly, the actual events of the trial and the Crucifixion
are not presented directly, but are made the subject of devotional
exhortations in which the sense of paradox predominates:

> See whear the Author of all life is dying:
> O fearefull day! He dead, what hope of liuing?
> See whear the hopes of all our liues are buying:
> O chearfull day! they bought, what feare of grieuing?
> Loue, loue for hate, and death for life is giuing:[11]

The suicide of Judas, stricken with despair and horror, is narrated directly in concrete terms, though the traitor is described
as besieged by demons and furies. Only in the hour of death
does Christ speak words of comfort to Mary, but this directly
reported speech merges at once into devotional commentary.

In the last book, Christ's Resurrection and Ascension, the
devotional element completely dominates. The Resurrection is
presented as it was manifested in its effects upon the world and

the creatures. The Ascension is described more directly in terms of the joy and praise which filled Heaven. The emphasis again falls upon Christ as conquering hero, and there is much sublime poetry in the description of the glories of Heaven; yet Fletcher cannot sustain the sublime note, but falls back upon the pastoral tone of the Song of Solomon to describe the union of Christ and the Church. Then he appeals to his brother Phineas, "the Kentish lad," to take over the heroic note, "that lately taught/ His oaten reed the trumpet's siluer sound—"[12]

There is very little that can be called heroic poetry in Fletcher's first major poem. He aspired to the noble genre, but he had no real conception of the form beyond a general appreciation of the requirements of dignity and elevation of style, and of classical devices such as the invocation, the extended descriptive passage, and the grand simile. What he wrote was a devotional poem in which he consciously strove to present the sublime element within a cosmic framework. Yet the cosmic drama was implied rather than exhibited directly; where action was required, as in the Temptation in the Wilderness, Fletcher fell back upon allegory. Indeed, all aspects of divinity, either of God or of Christ, were presented indirectly in allegorical form or devotional commentary. The relationship of divine action to the human situation is the main theme, but the connection is made not through action but through comment. Nevertheless, the elements of the Christian epic are all there in one form or another; even the Old Testament figures are brought in as analogies from time to time.[13] Yet we must conclude that Fletcher's strength as a poet lay primarily in his ability to charge a conceit or paradox with a metaphysical or baroque kind of intellectual excitement, and that he had practically no sense of the dramatic action required of heroic poetry.

Thomas Robinson's *Life and Death of Mary Magdalene,* written about 1620, is another poem which shows the influence

of Spenser and Du Bartas. Robinson does not directly aspire to
the nobility and elevation of the heroic genre, but his proposition
is couched in Virgilian form. He speaks of himself as a pastoral
poet, and explains that even humble subjects may have heavenly
significance:

> This bee the dity of my oaten reed,
> Too meane (alas!) such mysteries to tell:
> Yet heauens mirrour daine mee this one meed!
> In earthen vessles, heau'nly soules may dwell,
> And sandy caskets oft invest the pearle:
>   Aethereall states, and high Angellique traines,
>   (Blest bee the time!) haue sometime tooke the paines
> To visit Abells sonnes, poore, silly sheapeard-swaines.[14]

The poet plunges *in medias res* with an allegorical description
of the palace of Pleasure, of the stately dame herself, and the
many attendants, Flattery, Wantonness, Idleness, Jealousy, In-
constancy, Despair, Presumption, Envy, and so forth. Among
the revelers is Mary Magdalene, who lives only for the pleasure
of the moment and who is so beautiful that she is the object of
many rival suitors.

Conscience, however, visits Mary, and the occasion allows the
poet to describe Heaven with its spheres and planets. Mary at
first repents and rejects pleasure but suffers a relapse, and
Conscience returns this time in the form of a Fury with
"viperous" torments.[15] Robinson here adopted an element from
the hexameral set piece, but used the fearsome hag as an agent
of good rather than of evil. Mary is carried in imagination to
the gates of Hell, and the description that follows is in the
manner of the induction to the *Mirror*.[16] Mary undergoes a
sojourn in the cave of Melancholy and is then subjected to the
torments of Hell itself, but all this, the poet makes clear, is the
fantasy of a mind possessed.[17]

In the second part of the poem, Robinson temporarily drops

the allegory and in direct narrative describes the first meeting between Christ and Mary. Christ is pictured in terms of the Song of Solomon, but the poet also likens Christ to Perseus rescuing Andromede.[18] Pardoned of sin, Mary is taken to the palace of Wisdom and undergoes instruction by Repentance. The whole process is summed up in a crisp stanza:

> Desire's the cause of Sin; Sin, cause of greefe;
> Greife bids repent, Repentance brings forth teares;
> Teares, pities mooue, and pitty graunts releife
> That comforte, comforte hope, which nothings feares;
> Hope leades to faith, faith to the Sauiour reares:
>   Iesus, to blisse, his militants doth raize;
>   Blisse causes glory, glory ends in prayse;
> Prayse ends in him, that no beginninge knew, nor end of dayes.[19]

Much devotional material is worked into the account of Mary's repentance. The story of Mary's gift of precious ointment in the house of Simon is told in direct narrative, and Mary is again pardoned by Christ. The action concludes with Mary's lamentation over the death of Christ and her joy at seeing her risen Lord in the garden.

Robinson's interest in his subject is much less dominated by devotional concern than was Fletcher's. He takes great delight in embellishing his numerous descriptive passages with a wide range of detail drawn not only from the Bible but from the classics and contemporary secular literature. It is significant, however, that whenever he sets out to display the mind or inner conflict of Mary, he resorts to allegory of the medieval-Spenserian kind. When he presents the figure of Christ, he does so purely in the terms of the Bible and avoids any imaginative expansion of the situation. His main theme is not so much the conflict of good and evil in the cosmic setting as it is the regeneration of a soul through trial and suffering. The catalyst is Christ the

Redeemer and Example. It is curious that Robinson is at pains to emphasize the fact that his allegory is really a representation of the confused mind of Mary—an indication, perhaps, of the poet's desire to keep the imaginative aspects distinguished from the true Biblical elements. Mary thus remains a human example, and the sufferings she experiences are those of the soul seeking salvation. Just as he puts more stress upon the trial of the soul, so the poet puts less emphasis upon the cosmic setting of the action. Even the description of Hell is part of Mary's fantasy. There is no infernal council, no Satan, and only indirectly a vision of the glories of Heaven. The action remains firmly rooted in the earthly sphere throughout, and it is the human protagonist who is the center of the interest.

The poem is thus a kind of transition between the abstract portrayal of the soul's pilgrimage in the allegorical form and the concrete, heroic presentation of the worthy example found in the Old Testament narratives of Sylvester, Aylett, and Quarles. It belongs neither to one form nor the other in a decisive sense, and therefore seems ill-proportioned and inconclusive. Even Mary's relationship to Christ appears tenuous, recorded in the Bible but not imaginatively conceived by the poet. Indeed, if Mary had not been a New Testament figure and Christ had not been present, her repentance would still stand on its own as psychologically valid. In this sense the human action is closer to the kind of personal experience which Bunyan was to portray more vividly and in greater detail. In both, the Redemption by the sacrifice of Christ is theologically important and makes possible the regeneration of the human soul. But it is also the teaching and example of Christ which provides both the guide to salvation and the context of meaning for salvation. For both Robinson and Bunyan, however, the dramatic view of the cosmic conflict recedes before the intense interest in the immediate human experience. The hexameral setting tends to disappear as the emphasis falls more directly upon trial and suffering in the human sphere of action.

Joseph Beaumont's *Psyche*,[20] first published in twenty cantos in 1648, was revised and enlarged to twenty-four cantos by the author before his death in 1699, and was printed in final form by his son Charles in 1702. The theme is the pilgrimage of the soul, Psyche, through spiritual trial and suffering to salvation, conceived of as a kind of Neo-Platonic union with Christ the Bridegroom. Although there are many elements of Neo-Platonism throughout, such as the version of Joseph's vision or dream, the work is largely an elaboration of traditional materials in traditional forms. Beaumont was a resolute adherent of the Established Church, and much of his theology is thoroughly conservative. His treatment of the soul's pilgrimage is much more doctrinal in nature than Bunyan's. Psyche's actual experiences of the world are far less concrete and "physical" than those of Christian. Beaumont's allegory, though often vividly realized, is generally more abstract and spiritualized than Bunyan's. The world in which Psyche moves is primarily the world of the mind; Bunyan's Christian struggles through a world which is essentially everyday and real.

Beaumont's work, nevertheless, is the most fully developed example in pre-Miltonic Biblical narrative poetry of the fusing together of the main themes and forms of the period. Beaumont had a strong sense of the cosmic setting of the conflict between good and evil and repeatedly used the hexameral device of Satan and the infernal council to reinforce the various stages of Psyche's trial. Although the soul is the hero in the sense that it is the chief protagonist of the main action, the figure of Christ as Hero is constantly made parallel; so, actually, the work presents Christ as much as it does the human soul. Both Christ and Psyche are heroic examples, but Beaumont went even

farther: in the course of the instruction of Psyche by her
guardian angel, nearly all the major Old Testament figures are
brought in as specific examples of vices or virtues. We thus have
the whole range of traditional material brought together in a
long narrative, the framework of which is allegorical but which
develops in a pattern based on that of the classical epic. The
similarities to the *Faerie Queene* are obvious, but there is also
much similarity to Vida's *Christiad* in the narrative form. The
life of Christ, described in a series of episodes for the instruction
of Psyche, is, significantly, presented in direct narrative in the
manner of Vida. The progress of the soul, however, is always
portrayed allegorically. Actually, two forms of allegory are fused
to form a more elaborate connection between the cosmic and
the human spheres of action. The incidental allegory of the
hexameral theme, the personified vices, furies, and harpies,
represent not only temptations of the flesh and spirit but are
also the agents of Satan in a very real sense; the allegory of the
senses, states of mind, and qualities of mind or spirit provide
a second series of personifications acting either with or against
the demonic agents. The figure of Christ also has this double
aspect, both the active principle of good in the cosmic conflict
and the guiding principle of Divine Love in the human realm.

The main theme is the trial and preparation of the soul for
salvation or union with Christ. The action takes place in two
spheres: one, the cosmic, in which Satan and the forces of evil
strive for Psyche's defeat, and Psyche's guardian angel, Phylax,
prepares countermeasures; the other, the mind or spirit of the
human protagonist. Psyche is subjected to five main trials and
associated minor ones: Lust (Cantos I and II), Pride (Cantos
IV to VI), Heresy (Cantos XVIII and XIX), Persecution (Canto
XXII), and Spiritual Despair (Canto XXIII). After the second
test, the guardian angel presents the life of Christ in a series of
visions from the Birth in Canto VII to the Resurrection and

Ascension in Canto XV. There are thus nine long cantos devoted
directly and with little allegory to the whole life of Christ, and
it is in this section that the narrative mostly closely approximates
Vida's.

The first canto may be taken as representative of the way in
which Beaumont wove together the many traditional elements.
The proposition and invocation establish the comprehensiveness
of the design:

> Eternal Love, of sweetest Poetry
> The sweeter King, from thine high Mercies' Throne
> Deign to behold my prostrate Vow, and Me:
> No Muse, no Gods, but greater Thee alone
> I invocate; for both his heads full low
> Parnassus to thy Paradise doth bow.
>
> Thy Paradise, thro' whose fair Hills of Joy
> Those Springs of everlasting Vigor range,
> Which make Souls drunk with Heav'n, which cleanse away
> All earth from Dust, and Flesh to Spirit change.
> Wise loyal Springs, whose current to no Sea
> Its panting voyage ever steers, but Thee.[21]

The action begins with Satan addressing the infernal council.
Beaumont's Satan is a figure of considerable stature, proud,
undaunted, capable of devilish sophistry in accusing God and
Christ of tyranny and pride.[22] The motive for the seduction of
Psyche by the fury, Lust, is stated by Satan in perverted terms:

> Go then in God's name, but that God am I,
> And here my blessing on you all I deal.
> Catch but this Wench; and by that Victory
> We'll torture Christ more deeply than this Hell
> Doth you or Me, and so revenge the pain
> To which the Tyrant all brave Us doth chain.[23]

Lust prepares to adopt the disguise of a handsome young gallant,
but meanwhile Psyche's angel, Phylax, instructs his charge in

the dangers of lust by telling her the story of Joseph and Potiphar's wife. Included is an interesting statement of the basic concept of the rugged path of virtue to be followed by the Christian hero.

> Room, room enough: the King's High-way is less
> Kingly than this: the greatest Heroes who
> Have climb'd above the World, wish'd not to press
> Beyond these bounds. But be content to go
>> Where Saints, and where thy Lord before hath gone,
>> That thou mayst overtake him at his Throne.[24]

The story of Joseph is given full treatment in heroic narrative manner with some original touches elaborating Potiphera's pretense of being converted to Joseph's religion in order to win his sympathy.[25] The moral is intended as a forewarning of Psyche's own temptation by Lust:

> Thus Chastity's pure King his Champion sees
> Amply repaid; who having got Command
> Of his own Flesh and Blood, can rule with ease
> A Kingdom's reins. Mark well and understand,
>> Dear Psyche, this Narration's design.
>> The Case which here was His, may once be Thine.[26]

In each canto, much the same range of material is fused together; the connection between the cosmic setting, universal history, and the trials of the individual soul is constantly maintained. In Canto V, after Psyche has succumbed to the temptation of Pride in league with the Senses and Passions, a Masque of Bravery is presented in which Samson and David as well as many classical figures exemplify the fall of pride.[27] In Canto VI, the story of the Creation and the Fall further illustrates the foolishness of human pride and the necessity for humility. The problem of God's justice and mercy concludes the canto, and Beaumont arrives at an answer which is very similar to that of

Milton's: God's design is just, and although the Fall means sin
and suffering, the end is greater bliss for redeemed mankind:

> No Plot of Satan's spight must undermine,
> Or make a breach in His Creation's frame.
> Nature shall still proceed, and Heaven's Design
> Of Man's Felicity persist the same.
> Godlike it is indeed Fate's scales to turn,
> And make them Blest who to a Curse were born.
>
> Blest with more generous and victorious Bliss
> Than if the Curse's brand had never seal'd
> Them up in slavery to Death; thus his
> Renown more glorious is who wins the field
> After his Overthrow; than theirs who ne'r
> Disaster's game, and Conquest's booty were.[28]

The next nine cantos explain through the life of Christ the true
meaning of the triumph over evil in both the cosmic and the
human setting. The human trial and suffering of Christ are
also to be the examples for Psyche's further and more terrible
trials. The two cantos on heresy, however, have more than a
general significance, for they express Beaumont's own contempt
for the schismatic and dissenting elements in England. The
descriptions of the persecution of Psyche in Canto XXII are set
in a framework modeled on that of the Book of Job, but it is
apparent that Beaumont was portraying primarily the suffering
of the Established Church adherents in the period of the Civil
War and the Commonwealth. This canto, one which the poet
added after the Restoration, is too transparently polemical to
be wholly consistent with the large design of the rest.

Despite these shortcomings, Beaumont's conception is amaz-
ingly comprehensive and coherent when the various elements
are recognized in their true context and perspective. Although
the design was not developed with close adherence to classical
patterns, and adopts more from the Spenserian epic form than

from any other model, the poem contains elements from all the themes and forms that had been tried in the first half of the seventeenth century. There are many striking affinities with Du Bartas's hexameral epic.[29] The use of Old Testament examples such as Joseph suggests the work of Sylvester, Quarles, and Aylett. The story of the life of Christ resembles Vida's treatment most closely, but the use of allegory to portray the conflict of the soul is in the tradition of Spenser, Fletcher, and Robinson. There is, indeed, little that does not have some parallel with earlier examples of narrative poetry on sacred themes. What is most important, however, is that this apparently complex and abstruse work lies directly in the line which leads to Milton. The basic themes and concepts are fundamentally the same for all. The question is primarily where the emphasis was to fall. Beaumont chose to make the human soul, abstracted and refined so that the essential conflict would be clearly focused, the center of the action. Yet throughout the poem it is really Christ who is the Hero in the ultimate sense.

The concept of Christ as Hero is thus directly related to the concept of individual heroism in that both concepts are concerned with the struggle between good and evil. This relationship and the theme of spiritual warfare are perhaps nowhere more clearly stated than in the argument which precedes Edward Benlowes' *Theophila*:

The life of a true Christian is a continual Conflict. Each Act of the good Fight hath a Military Scene; and our Blessed SAVIOUR coming like a Man of War commands in Chief, under the FATHER, who hath layed Help upon One that is Mighty, by annointing him with the Holy GHOST and with Power. This World is his pitched Field; his Standard the Cross; his Colours Blood; his Armour Patience; his Battle Persecution; his Victory Death. And in a mystical Divinity his two-handed Sword is the Word and Spirit, which wounds and heals; and what is shed in this holy War is not Blood but Love; his Trumpeters are Prophets and Preachers; his Menacies

Mercies; and his Arrows Benefits: When he offers HIMSELF to us, He then invades us; His great and small Shot are Volies of Sighs and Groans; when we are converted we are conquer'd; He bindes when He embraceth us; In the Cords of Love He leads us Captives; and kills us into Life, when He crucifies the Old, and quickens in us the New Man.[30]

CHAPTER V

MILTON

IN THE preceding chapters we have seen that the concept of a
Christian epic based on Biblical subject matter was widespread enough in the first half of the seventeenth century
to be called one of the characteristic ideas, or ideals, of the age.
We have also seen that the various attempts to fulfill the ideal
met with serious obstacles created by the nature of the Biblical
materials and by the formal requirements of a genre borrowed
from classical pagan literature. These were obstacles which some
critics would call insurmountable. E. R. Curtius, commenting
on the Biblical epic in the broad perspective of Christian literature, had this to say: "Throughout its existence—from Juvencus
to Klopstock—the Biblical epic was a hybrid with an inner lack
of truth, a *genre faux*. The Christian story of salvation, as the
Bible presents it, admits of no transformation into pseudo-
antique form."[1] Stated in such broad terms, his judgment appears to be valid, though it would seem to lead to the conclusion
that even Milton's great epic was a brilliant but inherently
doomed experiment. The generalization needs to be qualified
in view of the special features which developed in the seventeenth-century English works of this kind. If the attempts of
Milton's predecessors to overcome the obstacles reveal anything
of significance, it is that their experiments helped to develop a
form of Biblical epic which was not a "hybrid" but a mutation
from the established classical pattern. It was not merely the
result of an artificial crossbreeding of Scripture and pagan epic,
but rather the working out of a distinct form of the heroic genre
which could best express vital Christian themes and concepts.

The poets at the beginning of the century possessed little

---

[1] For notes to chapter v see page 146.

more than a strong sense that the Bible provided the sublimest of subjects and the classical epic the noblest of forms, but as they strove to meet the more precise requirements of their broadly conceived ideal, they made changes and adjustments which led to the development of special themes within the traditional Christian pattern. These poets' works showed that no one of the three main types of Biblical subject matter could provide independently all the materials necessary for the epic portrayal of man's part in the Divine Plan, and that individual human acts of heroism were meaningful only when viewed within the scope of the Christian interpretation of universal history. None, however, were successful in giving these Christian themes the unity and coherence of the classical epic. What the poets had succeeded in doing was to make the archetypal pattern of temptation, fall, repentance, patience in suffering, and triumph through submission to the Will of God the chief characteristic of the concept of Christian heroism.

Milton's success lay in the fact that he was able to portray the full range of the cosmic drama while centering his design upon the First Temptation and Fall, the primal pattern for subsequent human struggle with evil. In the Second Temptation and victory of Christ lay the pattern of heroism for the individual, the promise of salvation to be won by the sorely tried Christian. In his epic poems, Milton successfully combined the significant elements of the three types of Biblical subject matter to produce the fullest possible perspective on the relationship of celestial and human events. Although Mr. Rajan was commenting only upon Milton's indebtedness to the hexameral tradition, his words can here be seen to apply to much more: "So when Milton came to write his epic he did not write it on a *tabula rasa*. Behind the thunder of his great argument were massed the reverberations of a literary past. Those echoes and cadences may not have been defined but Milton caught them in a defining harmony."[2]

To most seventeenth-century readers, Milton's subject matter would have been immediately recognizable as encompassing the traditional Christian view of the world and of universal history. For some readers the "novelty" of *Paradise Lost,* if such a word can be applied, would have lain in the fact that Milton was treating this sublime material in the form of the classical epic. For other readers who were familiar with the work of Du Bartas, Sylvester, Drayton, Quarles, Aylett, Beaumont, or Cowley, such an undertaking might not have seemed novel but rather a further attempt to write the long-sought-for Christian epic. To such readers it would not have appeared that Milton was breaking entirely new ground, but rather that he was bringing the main elements of the Christian tradition into clearer focus within the scope and unity of a full-scale epic design. There might have been much reason to doubt that he would succeed, but very little reason to question the worthiness or sublimity of his subject. Such was the attitude expressed by Andrew Marvell in his poem, "On Paradise Lost" (1674).

> When I beheld the Poet blind, yet bold,
> In slender Book his vast Design unfold,
> *Messiah* crown'd, God's Reconcil'd Decree,
> Rebelling Angels, the Forbidden Tree,
> Heav'n, Hell, Earth, Chaos, All; the Argument
> Held me a while misdoubting his Intent,
> That he would ruin (for I saw him strong)
> The sacred Truths to Fable and old Song
> (So *Sampson* grop'd the Temple's Posts in spite)
> The World o'erwhelming to revenge his sight.
>   Yet as I read, soon growing less severe,
> I lik'd his Project, the success did fear;
> Through that wide Field how he his way should find
> O'er which lame Faith leads Understanding blind;

Lest he perplex'd the things he would explain,
And what was easy he should render vain.

. . . .

But I am now convinc'd, and none will dare
Within thy Labours to pretend a share.
Thou hast not miss'd one thought that could be fit,
And all that was improper dost omit:
So that no room is here for Writers left,
But to detect their Ignorance or Theft.[2]

Marvell's first question, significantly, concerned the argument of the poem, "Held me a while misdoubting his Intent,/ That he would ruin .../ The sacred Truths. . . ." Milton's subject was no invention, but truth itself; his fear was that such truth might be confused with or reduced to the level of "Fable and old Song." Too slavish an imitation of classical form could easily have led to the artificial complexity that had marked other attempts to write a full-scale sacred epic. Marvell was probably aware that the vast design would be incomplete or distorted if the action were not properly proportioned to encompass all the important elements ranging through "Heav'n, Hell, Earth, Chaos, All." It can be imagined that Marvell would wonder, on reading the opening proposition of the work, how Milton intended to bring the full range of action into proper focus.

Marvell was completely reassured about Milton's intent and certain of his success. To a contemporary reader, then, Milton's vast design did satisfy the requirements of the traditional Christian view and did present the cosmic drama in all important aspects. Furthermore, the fact that Marvell made no attempt to explain Milton's argument suggests that he expected others to understand it, and that the real issue was the carrying out of such an exalted plan. It is worth considering, therefore, what Milton's proposition would have meant for the seventeenth-century reader who knew the essentials of Christian theology and could reasonably be expected to comprehend the design as a whole. Readers and critics of later ages have tended to emphasize as novel Milton's ambitious request of the Heavenly Muse that he "may assert Eternal Providence/ And justify the ways of God to men,"⁴ yet it is doubtful that a seventeenth-century reader would have found this new or pretentious. Probably he would have assumed that if Milton succeeded in portraying effectively the significance of the vast design, he would thereby have shown the justness of God's dealings with man in the most meaningful way.

Read thus, the proposition clearly stated that Milton's prime purpose was to show how in the Christian scheme of things temptation and suffering become the means by which Eternal Providence effects greater good. This could not be shown in human terms only. The first human fall from perfection had to be related to some greater action. The first question following the proposition posed the problem at once: "say first what cause/ Mov'd our Grand Parents in that happy State,/ . . . / Who first seduc'd them to that foul revolt?" (I, 28–33). The answer was terse and unequivocal: "Th' infernal Serpent" (I, 34). The action moved immediately from the human realm to the cosmic. The "Fable" thus became the conflict between good and evil in a universal sense. The human manifestations of this conflict were those of immediate concern for man; yet the larger issues were ultimately of the greatest importance, for the whole destiny of man was at stake. In both the human and the cosmic realms of action, Christ was the most transcendent figure, linking the two spheres in one greater action.

In the theological view of the cosmic action, Christ is the Son of God, but he is also the Creator, the Vanquisher of the rebellious angels, the Judge and the Advocate for fallen man. He is primarily the agent of good, just as Satan is the agent of evil. In the human action, Christ is the Divine Principle manifest in the flesh, undertaking the Atonement and Redemption in order to reconcile God and man and further to reduce the power of evil. Milton made clear, however, that this larger action was not a personal duel between Christ and Satan. It was only in Satan's perverted mind that such a duel seemed even possible. In Michael's words:

> Dream not of thir fight,
> As of a Duel, or the local wounds
> Of head or heel: not therefore joins the Son
> Manhood to Godhead, with more strength to foil
> Thy enemy; nor so is overcome
> *Satan,* whose fall from Heav'n, a deadlier bruise,
> Disabl'd not to give thee thy death's wound:
> Which hee, who comes thy Saviour, shall recure,
> Not by destroying *Satan,* but his works
> In thee and in thy Seed: nor can this be,
> But by fulfilling that which thou didst want,
> Obedience to the Law of God ...
>
> (XII, 386–397)

These, then, were the elements of the Christian drama of world history and mankind's destiny which the seventeenth-century reader of Milton's argument would expect to have presented to him—the elements which the Biblical narrative poets before Milton had usually seen in combination. The real question was not how clear this picture was in the mind of the poet, but where he placed the emphasis and how he proportioned the materials accordingly. If he chose to emphasize Creation or the Fall, he would feel constrained to complete the picture by presenting the course of history leading to Christ. If he were interested in portraying the human aspects of the conflict between good and evil by means of an Old Testament figure, he would have to show the action in the perspective of universal history between Creation and Christ. If he chose to treat the significance of Christ in New Testament themes, he would have to show the meaning of the Atonement and Redemption in both cosmic and human settings.

What then did Milton mean by his statement, "Things unattempted yet in Prose or Rhyme"? It was certainly not merely the fact that he was combining all the main elements of the Christian story in an epic poem for the first time. As this study has pointed out, these elements were already there in combination and had been treated in various ways by Milton's predecessors. Nor was it primarily the fact that Milton was the first to arrange these materials within a pattern modeled in part on the full-scale classical epic, for Cowley had attempted that, even if he had not completed the undertaking. Milton must have been aware that Cowley, although he took an Old Testament figure as his central protagonist, had established all the elements of the cosmic drama as part of the design in the first two books of the *Davideis*. It is possible, of course, that Milton was expressing a certain contempt for the earlier heroic poems, yet the word "unattempted" suggests that he had something different in mind.

Milton's title, *Paradise Lost,* and the proposition of the work both made clear that his main action was the Fall of man. He took the traditional view of the Fall as the first manifestation of evil in the newly created world of man and as the cause of all subsequent sin and suffering. In the total view, the action had broader implications than the immediate consequences of the entry of Sin and Death into the world. The implications extended out in space to encompass the universal human questions concerning the ways of God and the purpose of a Creation in which evil conflicts with good. The implications also extended on in time to involve questions regarding the destiny of mankind as a whole and the more immediate destiny of the individual soul. The entire cosmic drama was inevitably implied in the action of the Fall. By making the human action of Adam

and Eve central in his epic design, Milton supplied that unify-
ing focus of human interest which had been missing in the epic
survey of Creation and universal history by Du Bartas, and
which earlier poets had sought for in various Old or New Testament subjects. The full meaning of the struggle with evil was
thus made clear and comprehensible in human terms and in a
form suitably concrete and objective for an epic poem on the
classical model.

In *Paradise Lost,* therefore, Milton undertook to make explicit
the context in which his concept of the Christian hero was most
meaningful. If trial and suffering were the chief measures of
human heroism, then such trial had to be given a larger significance than that provided by human experience alone. Milton
had to portray the essential nature of the conflict between good
and evil in its fullest scope as it took place through all Creation
and all spheres of action: Heaven, Hell, Earth, and Chaos. By
undertaking this epic project, Milton was, at the same time,
presenting in objective form the answer to the profound question of God's purpose. The answer was implicit in the traditional Christian view, but the problem had been to present it
in an epic design that would keep the distinctions clear between
causes and effects and would make the connection between
the celestial and the human realms of action believable. The
figure of Christ was the necessary link. Christ was clearly the
Hero in the cosmic realm, the Conqueror of an evil summed
up in the figure of Satan. In the human realm, Christ was the
ultimate example and measure of Christian heroism, having
undergone humiliation and suffering in human terms for the
sake of man. Part of the problem, then, was to make Christ's
role in the epic action commensurate with his importance in the
Christian scheme, yet to avoid the difficulty of too direct a
presentation of the divine-human paradox.

By using the Temptation and the Fall for his central action,

Milton was able to avoid the problem of portraying Christ's suffering in human form, but could make clear Christ's role in the total action. In *Paradise Lost,* he portrayed the figure of Christ primarily as the Divine agent of good, the Son of God, the Victor over Satan in the Battle in Heaven, and the Creator of the new universe after the expulsion of the rebellious angels. In relation to the human action, Milton portrayed Christ as the Judge and Advocate, the instrument of both justice and mercy, the promised Redeemer through whose act of sacrifice God and man would be reconciled. These aspects are all those of Divinity operating in the cosmic realm rather than in the human. The human aspects of the Redemption, Christ's Passion in particular, Milton was able to present indirectly as ordained by God or as prophesied by Michael. In Book III, when the Son freely offered himself as ransom for man, the context was wholly cosmic, and it was the working out of Divine Providence that was stressed. Christ, then, can be said to be the archetypal heroic figure of *Paradise Lost.* He was not, however, a hero in any specifically human form. Milton relied heavily upon his readers' understanding of the traditional Christian view to supply the associations suggested in the proposition by the phrase, "one greater Man." As Milton himself stated in the *Christian Doctrine,*

How much better is it for us to know merely that the Son of God, our Mediator, was made flesh, that he is called both God and Man, and is such in reality;...Since however God has not revealed the mode in which this union is effected, it behoves us to cease from devising subtle explanations, and to be contented with remaining wisely ignorant.[5]

In *Paradise Regained,* however, Milton chose to emphasize the human aspects of Christ's role as much as possible. He could not avoid the divine element completely, but by restricting his action to the Temptation in the Wilderness, Milton was able to concentrate upon the struggle with evil almost wholly in the earthly sphere. Again, he relied upon his readers to supply the associations suggested in the proposition, "one man's firm obedience fully tried/ Through all temptation" (I, 4–5). Christ's victory over Satan was meant to represent an essentially human kind of victory, or at least one which, within human limitations, the Christian hero could imitate. There was very little emphasis upon the Redemption as such; indeed, Milton made Christ's victory over temptation appear the prototype of the greater cosmic triumph achieved by his sacrifice:

> now thou hast aveng'd
> Supplanted *Adam,* and by vanquishing
> Temptation, hast regain'd lost Paradise,
> And frustrated conquest fraudulent:
> (IV, 606–609)

It was in the example for man, however, that this earlier victory over Satan was most meaningful: "A fairer Paradise is founded now/ For *Adam* and his chosen Sons" (IV, 613–614). By portraying Christ's overcoming of the temptations of the world, Milton was able to provide a model for Christian heroism without risking entanglement in the mysteries of the divine-human paradox. Milton saw the temptations of evil in this world as the chief tests of the Christian hero's faith and fortitude, and therefore sought to portray the action in human terms. As Sir Herbert Grierson put it, commenting on the nature of seventeenth-century Puritanism: "There is something heroic, whatever we may think of the wisdom and the effects, in the thorough-going fashion in which the English Puritans asserted the other-worldly character of Christianity, while,... they also spurned all thought of a retreat from the world, affirmed that the world itself is the arena of the spiritual *askesis* and warfare which prepares the soul of man for the world to come."[6]

In both *Paradise Lost* and *Paradise Regained,* Christ's heroism is demonstrated in active forms as a victory over the arch-antagonist Satan, the figure objectifying all evil. Although there are paradoxical elements in the concept of Satan, they are not so critical in nature, for Satan was never a completely historical figure in the way that Christ was. The human imagination was thus relatively free to treat the manifestations of evil in human affairs as the work of Satan, and to embellish the concept with many extra-Biblical elaborations. Indeed, the figure of Satan was almost wholly extra-Biblical, having been developed primarily in the exegetical tradition as a means of making the conflict between good and evil more dramatic and awesome. The hexameral story of the Fall as set forth in Genesis had been developed into a conventional set piece in which Satan and the infernal council became the specific agents of temptation and discord in human affairs. When Milton undertook to portray the full scope of the cosmic conflict as the necessary context for the action in the human sphere, he had at hand an already developed figure of dramatic proportions suitable for his epic design. Milton was not one to underestimate the power of evil, or to restrain his imagination in depicting the magnitude of the struggle between good and evil where the Scriptures did not limit his conception.

The question of Satan's "heroism" has now perhaps been sufficiently argued on both traditional and modern grounds.[7] When viewed in terms of the traditional theology and the Christian story of the cosmic drama, however, the question loses much of its meaning. Satan is clearly evil, and evil must be recognized and rejected no matter in what tempting disguise it may appear. The very magnitude of evil may be awesome enough in the human realm, but when it is portrayed as Milton portrayed it on a cosmic scale, it may very well seem to possess epic features that could easily be misinterpreted as "heroic" in proportion. Milton was certainly faced with a critical artistic problem in his delineation of evil on this scale, and he had no classical model for a purely evil figure such as Satan. He could not risk making Satan too unequal an antagonist, even though God had fore-ordained the outcome, for then the heroism of Christ in both the cosmic and the human realms would be diminished, and the conflict would lose much of its epic effect. Milton had to endow Satan with sufficient grandeur for his role in the epic design, yet had to make clear that such grandeur was essentially false.

Although it is impossible to consider the problem fully here, it may be suggested briefly that Milton deliberately set out to contrast two kinds of heroism, one true, represented by Christ, the other false, represented by Satan. One is certainly aware of a kind of "heroic" quality in Satan, but if this quality is com-pared with the corresponding quality of heroism in Christ, the true measure of Satan's perverted grandeur becomes apparent. Professor M. Y. Hughes has pointed out[8] the growth of the Christian ideal of a contemplative type of magnanimity as the most nearly perfect virtue possessed by a Christian hero, and has contrasted it with the secular concept of magnanimity or "greatness of mind" which had also developed as the heroic ideal. The concept of "heroic martyrdom" required a new ap-praisal of the active virtues—pride, glory, power, fortitude—which had been traditionally associated with the classical epic hero, and with such figures as Hercules, who had long been seen as an example of a pagan hero faced with the problem of moral choice.[9] The distinction between the active and the contemplative forms of heroism depended upon the way in which heroic action was conceived, whether it took place in the arena of the world and society or in the mind or soul of the individual. The two types of heroism could be presented as complementing each other, or they could be contrasted in terms of their consequences for both the world and the spirit. Hughes cited Job[10] as one of the most popular of the figures exemplifying the contemplative form; the heroic action of Job was essentially one of patience and endurance leading to greater wisdom and faith, even though he was also rewarded in terms of earthly goods and favors. The Renaissance ideal, however, was to embody both forms in one hero, for it was desirable that the fruits of the contemplative life be manifested in the active life. For Milton, Christ represented both active and contemplative heroism in an ideal way. Satan's "heroic" qualities, however, he portrayed as essentially secular and worldly, based upon a perverse pride.

The Christian counterpart to pride is humility, not the humbleness of an inferior being but the calm assurance that limitations are balanced by the strength of partaking in a greater design for good. Milton emphasized this quality continually in *Paradise Lost* and *Paradise Regained* when he portrayed Christ in both the cosmic and the human realms of action. In Book III of *Paradise Lost,* the Son answered God's question concerning the need for divine atonement in these words:

> Behold mee then, mee for him, life for life
> I offer, on mee let thine anger fall;
> Account mee man; I for his sake will leave
> Thy bosom, and this glory next to thee
> Freely put off, and for him lastly die
> Well pleas'd, on me let Death wreck all his rage;
>
> . . . .
>
> His words here ended, but his meek aspect
> Silent yet spake, and breath'd immortal love
> To mortal men, above which only shone
> Filial obedience; as a sacrifice
> Glad to be offered, he attends the will
> Of his great Father.
>   (III, 236–241, 266–271)

In contrast, Satan's pride is made to appear foolish and self-deceiving, an unfounded confidence in his own limited powers. His only support was that of the inferior fallen angels, who had already tasted defeat and who, ironically, depended for their power upon the force of his false pride. The consequence of Satan's pride was perversion of right reason; hence, although Satan bitterly acknowledged the fruits of his disobedience in the soliloquy of Book IV, he could only reason that a return to obedience would be a "Short intermission bought with double smart" (IV, 102). On these grounds he refused to grant that hope of forgiveness was possible and determined upon a deliberate course of evil:

> So farewell Hope, and with Hope farewell Fear,
> Farewell Remorse: all Good to me is lost;
> Evil be thou my Good; by thee at least
> Divided Empire with Heav'n's King I hold
> By thee, and more than half perhaps will reign;
> As Man ere long, and this new World shall know.
>   (IV, 108–113)

Satan's apparent courage in the face of the absolute power of God turned out to be another self-deception. In the total action, he became merely an instrument carrying out God's design for greater good. In contrast, Christ's action in undertaking the Atonement and Redemption required a kind of courage directly opposed to that of Satan, since Christ sacrificed himself in full knowledge of the nature of human suffering. Although the outcome of Christ's conflict with Satan, Sin, and Death was foreordained, the dramatic nature of the conflict was nevertheless heightened on the human side, because it required the knowing sacrifice of the self to achieve a greater good—the most courageous act possible. The Christian concept of heroic martyrdom thus set up the courage of willingness to undergo sacrifice and suffering against the concept of courage based upon pride, honor, or unreasoning stubbornness.

In both the classical and the Christian view of the hero, strength of will was regarded as an essential characteristic. Milton offered, however, a profound contrast between Christ and Satan in this respect. Satan undoubtedly represented strength of will on an imposing scale, but even though he prided himself on reorganizing the fallen angels and building in Hell a seeming counterpart to the glories of Heaven, the reader knows that it was but empty pride and misdirected will. Satan's declamation, "Evil be thou my Good," was an obstinate perversion of all that was goodly in form and reasonable in true understanding. But Christ, in undertaking the Atonement, represented that creative strength of will which, because it was divine and goodly, sought to repair the form of the created world damaged by pride and disobedience.

In a similar way, greatness of mind had its secular and religious counterparts represented in Satan and in Christ. Much has been said of Satan's greatness of mind as a leader, but this quality could be regarded as a virtue only when a leader undertook a noble purpose. The grand manner, however, can fool, as Satan himself more or less admitted:

> *Disdain* forbids me, and my dread of shame
> Among the spirits beneath, whom I seduc'd
> With other promises and other vaunts
> Than to submit, boasting I could subdue
> Th' Omnipotent. Ay me, they little know
> How dearly I abide that boast so vain,
> Under what torments inwardly I groan:
> While they adore me on the Throne of Hell,
> With Diadem and Sceptre high advanc'd
> The lower still I fall, only Supreme
> In misery; such joy Ambition finds.
>   (IV, 82–92)

Satan's declamations are to be measured by the end or result, and there can be no doubt that it was a perverted purpose and a sorry end. Milton surely assumed that his readers were clear about that!

If Milton consciously depicted two kinds of epic heroism in Christ and Satan, one true and one false, what of Adam and Eve, the protagonists of the central action in *Paradise Lost*? Dryden felt that they could not rightly be called heroic, because they had sinned and the consequences were essentially tragic, both for themselves in the epic design and for mankind as a whole. Yet we know that Milton's conception of the epic action did not stop with the expulsion of man from Eden. The last two books of *Paradise Lost* function primarily to provide the reader with the view of universal history in which the cosmic drama continues to be played out. Milton's purpose was to make clear the full significance of trial and suffering as a necessary part of man's struggle with evil. By placing both the cause and the effect in the larger context, he gave the Christian hero the dignity of an important role in a conflict which was both human and cosmic. If Adam and Eve themselves were not essentially heroic, Milton could at least demonstrate that in repenting they had begun the task of seeking salvation, and that their descendants were capable of heroic action in the unceasing struggle with a Satan loose in the world.

After the Fall, man's powers were both limited and corruptible, but he retained virtue sufficient to make him worthy of Christ's act of Redemption. He could still be a combatant in his own limited way in the cosmic conflict with evil. Christ's sacrifice paid in human terms what Adam had forfeited, thus making possible a complete regeneration and salvation where before they had only been potential. But the descendants of Adam and Eve were still subject to Sin and Death. Milton, however, had Michael promise Adam "a paradise within thee, happier far" if he learned to distinguished good from evil and persevered in the cause of God. With the reassuring prophecy of Christ, Adam and Eve could accept the judgment and the expulsion from Eden, realizing the larger issues involved and the role which mankind could play.

The last two books of *Paradise Lost* were of prime importance in Milton's design, not because they were a conventional recapitulation of universal history, but because they provided the necessary context for Milton's concept of Christian heroism. For the theologian, the main purpose of the visions and prophecy given by Michael would be the promise of Christ's Redemption of mankind; yet Milton presented only a brief doctrinal outline of this dramatic turning point in Christian history. One reason lay in the fact that he had already developed the main features of the cosmic drama in the scenes in Heaven, and expected his readers to fill out the details of the Redemption for themselves. Another reason lay in the dramatic situation: Adam and Eve had to be prepared for the expulsion from Paradise so that they would go willingly, armed with faith in a happier future for mankind.

The last two books rounded out Milton's theme by applying the principles to be learned from the story of the cosmic drama to the concept of the Christian hero. The consequences of the Fall had been represented both directly and symbolically in Adam and Eve and in the effect upon Created Nature; the outline of universal history covering the Old Testament then served to exemplify the subsequent nature of human struggle with evil. It served also as a dramatic survey of the main forms of evil which man would experience in the course of history, and allowed Milton, through the words of Michael, to develop what might be considered a brief manual of conduct for the Christian hero. Adam himself was inspired to describe the role of human heroism in a passage which could stand as a kind of creed:

> Henceforth I learn, that to obey is best,
> And love with fear the only God, to walk

As in his presence, ever to observe
His providence, and on him sole depend,
Merciful over all his works, with good
Still overcoming evil, and by small
Accomplishing great things, by things deem'd weak
Subverting worldly strong, and worldly wise
By simply meek; that suffering for Truth's sake
Is fortitude to highest victory,
And to the faithful Death the Gate of Life;
Taught this by his example whom I now
Acknowledge my Redeemer ever blest.

(XII, 561–573)

Old Testament history had the further advantage for Milton of showing the inadequacy of man to make full restitution for the original sin without the intervention of Divine Grace and Mercy. Between the Fall and the Redemption, the Law was given through Moses as a necessary discipline to prepare man for "a better Cov'nant," but Sin and Death still reigned in the world, and fear rather than faith was often the means of discipline. Old Testament history was thus viewed as a necessary but imperfect stage in the regeneration of mankind, just as discipline was necessary for the individual soul in order to achieve a state of grace. Christ was the climax of the process, not because man had learned to live righteously by the Law, but because God had tempered justice with mercy and, with a greater good in view, had appointed a time for the promised Redemption. Milton wove together these two elements, man's limited efforts and God's Providence, in a passage which summed up the whole design of universal history:

Law can discover sin, but not remove,
Save by those shadowie expiations weak,
The blood of Bulls and Goats, they may conclude
Some blood more precious must be paid for Man,
Just for unjust, that in such righteousness

To them by Faith imputed, they may find
Justification towards God, and peace
Of Conscience, which the Law by Ceremonies
Cannot appease, nor Man the moral part
Perform, and not performing cannot live.
So Law appears imperfet, and but giv'n
With purpose to resign them in full time
Up to a better Cov'nant, ...

. . . .

And therefore shall not *Moses,* though of God
Highly belov'd, being but the Minister
Of Law, his people into Canaan lead;
But Joshua, whom the Gentiles *Jesus* call,
His Name and Office bearing, who shall quell
The adversary Serpent, and bring back
Through the world's wilderness long wander'd man
Safe to eternal Paradise of rest.

(XII, 290–314)

For Milton, faith in Christ's act of Redemption effectively super-
seded the Law, but before such faith was possible, Law was a
necessary discipline. Repentance was the first step, but before
Adam and Eve, or mankind, or the individual soul, could attain
complete and unshakable faith, instruction and discipline had
to be administered. For the Christian hero, the parallel of the
Old Testament examples of heroic trial and learning through
suffering would still be meaningful and applicable. Man still
had to prove his faith in the imputed righteousness bestowed
by Christ, and had to strive mightily for the salvation which was
his goal.

Milton was able to show not only the original cause of sin
and suffering but also the human strengths and weaknesses
which were to determine man's ability to struggle with evil.
In Books XI and XII, the nature of that struggle was foreshadowed in the visions and prophecy of Old Testament history leading to Christ. In the Cambridge Manuscript,[11] in the

third and fourth drafts of his proposed drama on the Fall, Milton had outlined an allegorical dumb show or masque by means of which Adam and Eve were to be instructed in the consequences of their sin. In *Paradise Lost,* however, Milton rejected allegorical apparatus in favor of direct examples from Old Testament history. The "mask of all the evills of this life & world"[12] in the fourth draft became in effect the visions of Book XI, covering envy and murder in the vision of Cain and Abel, diseases and various forms of death in the vision of the lazar house, the corruption of good by evil in the mating of progeny of Cain and Seth, the destruction and chaos of war, and the luxury, riot, and degeneracy of the race of man by the time of Noah and the Flood. Such visions of evil not only had the effect of humbling Adam still further but also enabled Milton to point out the false nature of worldly glory and prowess:

> Those whom last thou saw'st
> In triumph and luxurious wealth, are they
> First seen in acts of prowess eminent
> And great exploits, but of true virtue void;
> Who having spilt much blood, and done much waste
> Subduing Nations, and achiev'd thereby
> Fame in the World, high titles, and rich prey,
> Shall change thir course to pleasure, ease, and sloth,
> Surfeit, and lust, till wantonness and pride
> Raise out of friendship hostile deeds in Peace.
>
> (XI, 787-796)

In Book XII, Milton dropped the device of the vision and substituted prophecy by Michael, who outlined the subsequent Old Testament history until the coming of Christ. There is a certain parallel in this outline with the structure of Du Bartas's *Second Weeke* in that Milton concentrated upon six main stages or cardinal events: Nimrod and the Tower of Babel, Abraham, Moses, David, the Exile, and finally Christ. Milton had a special interest in Nimrod, the subject of Du Bartas's Second Part of the Second Day, as the symbol of tyranny and ambition for power leading to the loss of rational liberty. Du Bartas had treated both Abraham and Moses in the Third Day, but Milton elaborated upon the role of Moses as the giver of the Law. Milton's next three stages correspond to those of Du Bartas, although Milton considerably reduced them; it was unnecessary that he elaborate them because they served only to represent the course of history and to provide a few cardinal examples of human heroism. For the reader, Milton intended the last two books to draw the attention down from the sublime and cosmic aspects to the immediate world in which the Christian hero had to face the grim reality of evil and undergo the trials and suffering of human life.

In view of Milton's interest in delineating the true nature of Christian heroism, it is understandable that he should turn to the most human aspect of Christ in *Paradise Regained*. In this brief epic on the model of Job, Milton deliberately chose not to deal with the whole of Christ's life or even with the Passion. Instead, he made the Temptation represent the larger act of Atonement and Redemption in a way that was most exemplary for the human followers of Christ. The divine aspects he reduced to a minimum in order to emphasize the fact that victory over Satan's temptations in this world was both necessary and possible for the man of faith and fortitude. He provided a deliberate contrast with the worldly concept of heroism early in the poem when he revealed Christ meditating upon his contest with evil:

> yet this not all
> To which my Spirit aspir'd, victorious deeds
> Fram'd in my heart, heroic acts; one while
> To rescue *Israel* from the Roman yoke,
> Then to subdue and quell o'er all the earth
> Brute violence and proud Tyrannic pow'r,

Till truth were freed, and equity restor'd:
Yet held it more humane, more heavenly, first
By winning words to conquer willing hearts,
And make persuasion do the work of fear;

(I, 214–223)

For Milton the real victory over evil was to be won in the
individual human spirit, not in the larger area of worldly pomp
and glory. The Temptation therefore became for Milton the
most humanly significant event of Christ's life and ministry,
for it provided the clearest model of heroic faith and fortitude—
"deeds/ Above Heroic, though in secret done" (I, 14–15). Although the Passion was theologically more important, Milton
recognized the profound difficulty of making Christ's suffering
and sacrifice for the cosmic requirements of the Atonement a
model for human action. In the early, unfinished poem, *The
Passion,* Milton had called Christ "Most perfect *Hero,* tried in
heaviest plight / Of labours huge and hard, too hard for human
wight" (lines 13–14). In *Paradise Regained* he deliberately chose
to emphasize labors that were *not* too hard for human endeavors
or were at least possible, given enduring faith and fortitude.

In the figure of the tempted Christ, Milton faced his most
formidable artistic challenge, for if the temptations of this world
culminating in those of learning were to be meaningful in human terms, Milton could not afford to emphasize the divinity
of Christ, yet he could not present him as simply human. He
represented Christ, therefore, as the "exalted man," the Example
for the followers who must be armed with virtue, wisdom, and
faith for the trials of this world. Professor D. C. Allen concluded
that Milton failed in the artistic task of keeping the divine and
human natures of Christ distinct yet unified in the theological
sense, but he added that Milton came closer to portraying the
concept poetically than any other poet or theologian who had
attempted it before.[18] He pointed out that Milton used two dra-

matic devices to emphasize the human nature of Christ: the meditations of Christ in which humanity prevailed, and the doubts raised for the reader by Satan's questions about divine favor. "When Christ is alone, he is human; when he is confronted by Satan, he assumes divinity or, at least, is raised above humanity. On these occasions Christ not only knows himself, but remembers the long history of his opponent both in Heaven and in earth."[14] Professor Arnold Stein has given this aspect of Christ's action a kind of psychological interpretation, seeing it as essentially the human process of searching for the past within the mind in order to gain self-knowledge and prepare for the great task ahead.[15] The knowledge that Christ gained in this trial was a full realization of his divine nature and purpose. Certainly, as Satan's devices failed one by one, Christ revealed greater and greater assurance of his role until the final futility of Satan's last desperate measure was shown in the calm and damning indictment: "Thou shalt not tempt the Lord thy God." The action had progressed from the essentially human area of temptation to the final affirmation of the sublimity of Christ as the center of universal history and as Victor in the cosmic battle.

The paradox of Christ's nature was one which Milton's art could not wholly avoid. Christ as the Second Adam could never be completely separated from Christ the Son of God. The problem was exemplified in the first speech of God, explaining the paradox to the heavenly hosts:

> But first I mean
> To exercise him in the Wilderness;
> There he shall first lay down the rudiments
> Of his great warfare, ere I send him forth
> To conquer Sin and Death the two grand foes,
> By Humiliation and strong Sufferance:
> His weakness shall o'ercome Satanic strength
> And all the world, and mass of sinful flesh;
> That all the Angels and Ethereal Powers,

> They now, and men hereafter, may discern
> From what consummate virtue I have chose
> This perfect Man, by merit call'd my Son,
> To earn Salvation for the Sons of men.
> (I, 155–167)

Here the pattern of victory through trial, humiliation, suffering, and fortitude parallels the pattern which Michael taught Adam in *Paradise Lost*. Though Milton stressed Christ's role as "perfect Man," the fact remains that God ordained the victory. The host of Heaven, praising God's justice and mercy, saw the action primarily in its cosmic context:

> Victory and Triumph to the Son of God
> Now ent'ring his great duel, not of arms,
> But to vanquish by wisdom hellish wiles.
> The Father knows the Son; therefore secure
> Ventures his filial Virtue, though untried,
> Against whate'er may tempt, whate'er seduce,
> Allure, or terrify, or undermine.
> (I, 173–179)

Doubt and irresolution would be major human weaknesses in such a trial, and Milton skillfully suggested the presence of these failings, not in Christ, but in Andrew and Simon who began to doubt their faith in the Messiah merely because of Christ's prolonged absence (II, 6–57). Such human weakness was an element in the struggle with evil which Milton recognized as a necessary consequence of the first Fall, and a factor which made Christian heroism not only a matter of victory over external evil but also a question of conquering the limitations inherent in man. Allegory had long been a means of portraying this internal conflict, but Milton preferred to represent the struggle in realistic and historically true examples drawn from the Bible. Milton's vision of the reality of evil in the world, ranging from the full sweep of the cosmic drama to the actions of individual human beings, did not allow him to translate the literal truths of the Bible account of this struggle into moral or mystical abstractions in allegorical form. The temptation to indulge in a Spenserian form must have been strong, but the fact that he kept his narration consistently objective is a measure of his control of both form and subject.

Milton did have precedents for a realistic portrayal of this internal struggle in the widespread use of Old Testament figures in the narrative poetry of the first half of the century. If the figure of Christ as a model for human heroism had always been difficult to present, the Old Testament figures, types of Christ, had been viewed as exemplifying the struggle with evil in the purely human realm of action. Milton probably saw in the Old Testament figure of Samson not only a type of Christ but also a human figure representative of both the external and the internal conflict with evil. The Christ of *Paradise Regained* had provided the ideal model of victory over evil, but Samson could illustrate more clearly the human actualities and the possibilities of victory over the worst of man's weaknesses, doubt and spiritual despair.

Samson Agonistes is tragic drama, not heroic narrative,[16] but it complements Milton's treatment of the concept of Christian heroism in full-scale and brief epic forms. Most important is the fact that Samson could be made a purely human example of one aspect of the "Christian" hero. Although the associations of Christ and Samson in the figural interpretation were still vital when Milton wrote the tragedy, the growing rationalism of the latter half of the century allowed him to put greater emphasis upon Samson as an independent historical figure. Moreover, Milton did not stress the larger context of the cosmic drama nor give the human figure of Samson the support of the larger meaning of Christ in universal history. Samson was an example of tragic heroism in which the internal conflict with evil had to be resolved without divine support other than faith and fortitude. Though Samson was an instrument of Providence, his end was tragic because before Christ's act of Redemption there could be no Christian sense of salvation. But Milton was able to show that faith and submission to the Will of God, together with fortitude in trial and suffering, were the true measures of the Christian hero.

In *Paradise Lost* Milton had portrayed on an epic scale the universal struggle with evil and had shown the full consequences for man of the first Temptation and Fall. In the last two books of the epic he had outlined the nature of the human role in the cosmic drama and had provided in rather doctrinal terms a manual for the Christian hero. In *Paradise Regained* he had concentrated upon the most dangerous worldly temptations and had portrayed in Christ's human experience the perfect model for human heroism. In both works he showed that trial and patient endurance of suffering were the means by which victory over evil could be achieved. The significance for the individual Christian soul was clear. Just as in the cosmic drama the first Fall was paradoxically the means through which Providence worked to achieve a larger measure of good, so, for the individual, the fall into temptation and sin with its consequent suffering could become the means of attaining greater spiritual strength. In the last analysis, Milton's strong religious convictions led him to emphasize the need for victory over evil first within the individual.

Milton's epic poems can thus be viewed as a culmination of the search which took place in the first half of the century for the ideal Christian epic form and, as a consequence, for the most effective delineation of Christian heroism. The search had led Milton's English predecessors in heroic narrative poetry to try various combinations of form and subject matter. Central to all these experiments was the Christian perception of the correspondence between the human drama and the working out of Providence in universal history. These were the materials with which Milton worked, but it lay in the power of his genius to achieve a more comprehensive design and a more effective proportion than had been attained before. These materials were all parts of the traditional Christian view, but Milton was able to utilize them in different ways to portray objectively his concept of the Christian hero. Taken together they provided a dramatic picture of the Divine Plan in which the individual human being is dignified by a role that makes him not only the passive instrument of Providence but also an agent of good in winning victory over himself.

Milton's concept of the Christian hero recognized human limitations and rejected any notion of an easy victory by virtue of divine intervention. For Milton, Christ's Atonement and Redemption did not automatically assure man of victory over evil, but rather made it possible for man to become in part the agent of his own salvation. That Milton had long considered the problem of Christian heroism can be seen in this statement in *Areopagitica*:

Good and evil we know in the field of this world grow up together almost inseparably; and the knowledge of good is so involved and interwoven with the knowledge of evil, and in so many cunning resemblances hardly to be discerned, ... And perhaps this is that doom which Adam fell into of knowing good and evil; that is to say, of knowing good by evil.

As therefore the state of man now is; what wisdom can there be to choose, what continence to forbear, without the knowledge of evil? He that can apprehend and consider vice with all her baits and seeming pleasures, and yet abstain, and yet distinguish, and yet prefer that which is truly better, he is the true wayfaring Christian.... Assuredly we bring not innocence into the world, we bring impurity much rather; that which purifies us is trial, and trial is by what is contrary.[17]

Perhaps the most striking aspect of the Biblical heroic poetry of the first half of the seventeenth century, the aspect that Milton saw and utilized most effectively, was the way in which the hexameral themes of the cosmic setting and the concept of universal history contributed to an understanding of human affairs. For the Christian epic conception, the human hero was not complete in himself, but depended upon the greater significance of Christ in the context of universal action. Both the Christian themes and the requirements of epic form, at first conceived in terms of classical models, had worked together to create a special kind of heroic genre, and to demand an ideal of Christian heroism which was larger than life-size. In the cosmic setting, only Christ could be such a hero; in the earthly setting, the human hero had to be as close as possible to the example of Christ. For the Christian, mere earthly glory had eventually to be transcended by the celestial. The emphasis upon the cosmic aspect was thus necessary to provide a more glorious meaning for the suffering and humiliation borne by the Christian hero. The concept of heroic martyrdom could not be understood unless it was seen in the full perspective of the Christian vision of the struggle between good and evil. Of all the human figures in the Bible, Job perhaps came closest to representing the ideal of heroic faith, patience, and fortitude in the face of trial and suffering. Milton had Christ in *Paradise Regained* (III, 60–67) reply to Satan's offer of worldly glory and fame in these significant words:

> This is true glory and renown, when God
> Looking on the Earth, with approbation marks
> The just man, and divulges him through Heaven
> To all his Angels, who with true applause
> Recount his praises; thus he did to *Job,*
> When to extend his fame through Heaven and Earth,
> As thou to thy reproach mayst well remember,
> He asked thee, hast thou seen my servant *Job?*

APPENDIX

APPENDIX

Classification by Dominant Form

A. Discursive

    1. *The Divine Workes and Weekes of Du Bartas,* trans. Sylvester, 1605.

    2. *Christ's Victorie* (Books III, IV), G. Fletcher, 1610.

    3. *Doomes-day,* Alexander, 1614.

    4. *The Glasse of Time,* Peyton, 1620, 1623.

    5. *Hadassa* (Meditations only), Quarles, 1621.

    6. *Job Militant* (Meditations only), Quarles, 1624.

    7. *A Feast for Wormes* (Meditations only), Quarles, 1626.

    8. *Doomesday,* Mure, 1628.

    9. *The Perfect-Cursed-Blessed Man,* J. Fletcher, *ca.* 1629.

    10. *The Historie of Samson* (Meditations only), Quarles, 1631.

B. Allegorical

    1. *Christ's Victorie* (Books I, II), G. Fletcher, 1610.

    2. *The Life and Death of Mary Magdalene,* Robinson, *ca.* 1620.

    3. *The Apollyonists,* P. Fletcher, 1627.

    4. *Psyche,* Beaumont, 1648; rev. and enl. 1702.

    5. *Theophila,* Benlowes, 1652.

C. Classical Heroic

    1. *Moses His Birth and Miracles,* Drayton, 1604.

    2. *Judith,* Du Bartas, trans. Sylvester, 1614.

    3. *Job Triumphant in His Triall,* Sylvester, 1620.

    4. *The Maiden's Blush,* trans. Sylvester, 1620.

    5. *Hadassa* (Narrative only), Quarles, 1621.

    6. *Susanna,* Aylett, 1622.

    7. *Joseph,* Aylett, 1623.

    8. *Job Militant* (Narrative only), Quarles, 1624.

    9. *A Feast for Wormes* (Narrative only), Quarles, 1626.

    10. *David and Golia,* Drayton, 1630.

    11. *Noah's Flood,* Drayton, 1630.

    12. *The Historie of Samson* (Narrative only), Quarles, 1631.

    13. *David's Heinous Sin, David's Hearty Repentance, David's Heavy Punishment,* Fuller, 1631.

    14. *Jonathan,* Alexander, 1637.

15. *The Suspicion of Herod,* Crashaw, 1646.
16. *Davideis,* Cowley, 1656.
17. *Paradise Lost,* Milton, 1667.
18. *Paradise Regained,* Milton, 1671.

With these, the following rare works should be noted:

> *Eustathia, The Constancie of Susanna,* Robert Roche, 1599.
> *Harmonies on the First and Second Books of Samuel,* Andrew Willet, 1614.
> *Joseph, Egypt's Favorite,* Sir Francis Hubert, 1631.
> *The History of Joseph,* Thomas Salisbury, 1636.

It should be noted also that George Sandys' *Paraphrase of Job,* 1638, belongs more to the category of translation than of heroic treatment, but it does possess some heroic features. Zachary Boyd's *Zion's Flowers* (Joseph, Dinah, David and Goliath, Jonah), written before 1626, presents the material in the form of dialogue.

CLASSIFICATION BY SUBJECT MATTER

A. Hexameral

1. *The Divine Workes and Weekes of Du Bartas,* trans. Sylvester, 1605.
2. *Doomes-day,* Alexander, 1614.
3. *The Glasse of Time,* Peyton, 1620, 1623.
4. *The Apollyonists* (Assembly in Hell), P. Fletcher, 1627.
5. *Doomesday,* Mure, 1628.
6. *Noah's Flood,* Drayton, 1630.
7. *The Suspicion of Herod* (Assembly in Hell), Crashaw, 1646.
8. *Paradise Lost,* Milton, 1667.

(Both Beaumont's *Psyche* and Benlowes' *Theophila* have sections of hexameral material, principally concerned with the temptation and fall of Adam and Eve.)

B. Old Testament

1. *The Historie of Judith,* Du Bartas, trans. Hudson, 1584.
2. *Moses His Birth and Miracles,* Drayton, 1604.
3. *The Divine Workes and Weekes of Du Bartas* (*Second Weeke,* Third and Fourth Days), trans. Sylvester, 1605.

4. *Judith*, Du Bartas, trans. Sylvester, 1614.
5. *Job Triumphant in His Triall*, Sylvester, 1620.
6. *The Maiden's Blush*, trans. Sylvester, 1620.
7. *Hadassa*, Quarles, 1621.
8. *Susanna*, Aylett, 1622.
9. *Joseph*, Aylett, 1623.
10. *Job Militant*, Quarles, 1624.
11. *A Feast for Wormes*, Quarles, 1626.
12. *David and Golia*, Drayton, 1630.
13. *The Historie of Samson*, Quarles, 1631.
14. *David's Heinous Sin, David's Hearty Repentance, David's Heavy Punishment*, Fuller, 1631.
15. *Jonathan*, Alexander, 1637.
16. *Davideis*, Cowley, 1656.

C. New Testament
1. *Christ's Victorie*, G. Fletcher, 1610.
2. *The Life and Death of Mary Magdalene*, Robinson, *ca.* 1620.
3. *The Suspicion of Herod*, Crashaw, 1646.
4. *Psyche*, Beaumont, 1648.
5. *Theophila*, Benlowes, 1652.
6. *Paradise Regained*, Milton, 1671.

NOTE: Joseph Fletcher's *Perfect-Cursed-Blessed Man, ca.* 1629, covers both the Temptation and Fall of Adam and Eve and the Passion of Christ as the necessary means of Atonement and Redemption. It is thus equally hexameral and New Testament in its subject matter.

NOTES

NOTES TO THE INTRODUCTION
(Pages 1–5)

[1] W. H. Auden, *The Enchafèd Flood*, p. 93.

[2] Robert M. Adams, *Ikon: John Milton and the Modern Critics*, p. 129.

[3] William Haller, *The Rise of Puritanism*, p. 23.

[4] Throughout this study, I have followed the example of Arnold Williams in his discussion of these materials in *The Common Expositor*, using the form "hexameral" rather than "hexaemeral."

NOTES TO CHAPTER I
(Pages 6–32)

[1] See Rosemond Tuve, *A Reading of George Herbert*; Erich Auerbach, *Mimesis*; and Northrup Frye, "The Typology of *Paradise Regained*," *MP*, LIII, 227–238.

[2] See Lily B. Campbell, "The Christian Muse," *Huntington Library Bulletin*, No. 8 (1935), 29–70.

[3] Text in G. G. Smith, *Elizabethan Critical Essays*, I, 154.

[4] *Ibid.*, p. 155.

[5] *Ibid.*, p. 158.

[6] *Ibid.*, p. 179.

[7] See E. M. W. Tillyard, *The English Epic and Its Background*, chaps. v, vi.

[8] J. E. Spingarn, ed., *Critical Essays of the Seventeenth Century*, II, 5.

[9] That is, the pagans, neither Christian nor Jewish; this is clearly a reference to the classical pagan literature and the blind imitation of the *form* of this literature without thought to the difference in *subject*.

[10] Spingarn, *op. cit.*, p. 30.

[11] *Ibid.*, p. 59.

[12] *Ibid.* For a discussion of the influence of the seventeenth-century "heavenly" poetry of the Biblical, particularly hexameral, kind upon eighteenth-century practice, see Josephine Miles, "The Sublime Poem," in *The Image of the Work*, pp. 59–85.

[13] Spingarn, *op. cit.*, II, 88 f.

[14] *Ibid.*, p. 89.

[15] *Ibid.*, p. 90.

[16] Don M. Wolfe, ed., *Complete Prose Works of John Milton*, I, 813.

[17] *Ibid.*, pp. 813–814.

[18] R. A. Sayce, *The French Biblical Epic in the Seventeenth Century*.

[19] *Ibid.*, p. 160 f.

[20] See Arnold Williams, *The Common Expositor*, chap. i.

[21] For a survey of medieval exegesis, see Beryl Smalley, *The Study of the Bible in the Middle Ages*.

[22] See F. M. Krouse, *Milton's Samson and the Christian Tradition*.

[23] See Elizabeth M. Pope, *Paradise Regained: The Tradition and the Poem*.

[24] Campbell, *op. cit.*

[25] George Puttenham, *The Arte of English Poesie*, p. 54.

[26] Francis Sabie, *The Olde Worlde's Tragedie*, University Microfilm Series, no. 15401, Sig. D2r.

[27] *Ibid.*, Sig. Fv.

[28] E. R. Curtius, *European Literature and the Latin Middle Ages*, p. 167 f.

[29] See M. Y. Hughes, "The Christ of *Paradise Regained* and the Renaissance Heroic Tradition," *SP*, XXXV (1938), 254–277.

[30] Auerbach, *op. cit.*, p. 16.

[31] See Don Cameron Allen, *The Legend of Noah*, Illinois Studies in Language and Literature, vol. 33, nos. 3–4 (1949).

[32] See Ernest L. Tuveson, *Millennium and Utopia*.

[33] R. Blanchard, ed., *Tracts and Pamphlets by Richard Steele*, p. 36.

[34] William Haller, *The Rise of Puritanism*, p. 23.

[35] *Ibid.*, p. 34.

NOTES TO CHAPTER II
(Pages 33–52)

[1] Sir Walter Raleigh, *The History of the World*, Book I, chap. v, p. 40.

[2] Grant McColley, *Paradise Lost*, p. 185.

[3] *Ibid.*, p. 10.

[4] U. T. Holmes, ed., *The Works of . . . Du Bartas*, I, 111.

[5] Thomas Lodge, "To the Reader," *A Learned Summarie upon . . . Bartas*, no sig.

[6] *Ibid.*, Sig. A4r.

[7] Holmes, *op. cit.*, III, 119.

[8] *Ibid.*, I, 219.

[9] Joshuah Sylvester, *The Divine Workes and Weekes of Du Bartas*, I, lines 214–221.

[10] *Ibid.*, "The Handy-Crafts," line 358 f.

[11] *Ibid.*, "Tropheis," lines 624–799.

[12] *Ibid.*, lines 17–23.

[13] *Ibid.*, "The Imposture," marginal note, line 242.

[14] *Ibid.*, line 153 f.

[15] *Ibid.*, "The Captaines," line 1230 f.

[16] *Ibid.*, "The Law," line 844 f.

[17] Cited in J. M. McBryde, Jr., "A Study of Cowley's *Davideis*," JGP, II, no. 4 (1898), 484.

[18] Text in Carmelite Brothers, *Satan*, p. 22.

[19] W. M. Bloomfield, *The Seven Deadly Sins*, p. 222.

[20] Sylvester, *op. cit.*, "The Imposture," line 150 f.

[21] R. A. Sayce, *The French Biblical Epic . . .*, p. 170.

[22] *Ibid.*, p. 175.

[23] Abraham Cowley, *The Complete Works*, II, 79.

[24] Sir William Alexander, *Doomes-day*, p. 231.

[25] *Ibid.*, "Introduction," p. xix.

[26] Thomas Peyton, *The Glasse of Time . . .* (1620, 1623), p. 44.

[27] See *ibid.*, pp. 140–142, for various opinions on skin pigmentation.

[28] Sir William Mure, *Doomesday*, p. 178.

NOTES TO CHAPTER III
(Pages 53–79)

[1] Hallett Smith, *Elizabethan Poetry* (Cambridge, Mass.: Harvard University Press, 1952), chap. vi.

[2] E. M. W. Tillyard, *The English Epic and Its Background*, pp. 356–359.

[3] Joshuah Sylvester, *The Divine Workes and Weekes of Du Bartas*, Vol. II, Book VI, line 149 f.

[4] Described in R. A. Sayce, *The French Biblical Epic . . .*, p. 68.

[5] Michael Drayton, *The Works*, Vol. III, Book II, line 625 f.

[6] *Ibid.*, Book III, line 61 f.

[7] Thomas Fuller, *David's Heinous Sin, David's Hearty Repentance, David's Heavy Punishment.*

[8] *Ibid.*, p. 204.

[9] *Ibid.*, p. 203.

[10] *Ibid.*, p. 213.

[11] *Ibid*, p. 237.

[12] Sylvester, *op. cit.*, II, line 51 f.

[13] *Ibid.*, line 961 f.

[14] *Ibid.*, line 1076.

[15] Robert Aylett, *Joseph*, p. 2.

[16] *Ibid.*, p. 15.

[17] *Ibid.*, p. 33.

[18] *Ibid.*, p. 50.

[19] *Ibid.*, pp. 18–19.

[20] *Ibid.*, p. 61 f.

[21] *Ibid.*, p. 65.

[22] *Ibid.*, p. 95.

[23] Aylett paraphrases the passage "I know that my Redeemer liveth" as part of Jacob's dying speech.

[24] Sylvester, *op. cit.*, II, 47.

[25] *Ibid.*, p. 147.

[26] *Ibid.*

[27] Francis Quarles, *The Works*, II, 82.

[28] *Ibid.*, II, 98.

[29] *Ibid.*, II, 162.

[30] *Ibid.*, II, 168.

[31] *Ibid.*, II, 6.

[32] J. M. McBryde, Jr., "A Study of Cowley's *Davideis*," *JGP*, II, no. 4 (1898), 454–527.

[33] J. E. Spingarn, ed., *Critical Essays of the Seventeenth Century*, II, 86–87.

[34] *Ibid.*, p. 86.

[35] Abraham Cowley, *The Complete Works*, II, lines 780–850.

[36] *Ibid.*, lines 269–328.

[37] *Ibid.*, lines 456–837.

[38] Samuel Johnson, *The Lives of the English Poets* (1783), I, 84.

[39] Cowley, *op. cit.*, lines 1–12.

[40] See, for example, Tillyard, *op. cit.*, p. 426.

NOTES TO CHAPTER IV
(Pages 80–106)

[1] Joseph Fletcher, *The Perfect-Cursed-Blessed Man*, p. 110.

[2] Vida, *Christiad*, p. 315.

[3] Cited in Gustaf Aulén, *Christus Victor*, p. 33.

[4] A fourth aspect of Christ, his role as Creator, should be mentioned because it was traditionally part of the concept of the cosmic drama, but this aspect was one which only Milton was to make part of the epic action in *Paradise Lost*. Du Bartas described Creation as decreed by the Trinity acting as One.

[5] Vida, *op. cit.*, p. 5.

[6] *Ibid.*, p. 15.

[7] Abraham Cowley, *The Complete Works*, Vol. II, Book I, lines 117–214.

[8] Giles Fletcher, *The Complete Poems*, p. 132.

[9] *Ibid.*, p. 157.

[10] *Ibid.*, p. 201.

[11] *Ibid.*, p. 206.

[12] *Ibid.*, p. 242.

[13] *Ibid.*, Book I, st. 16 and 34; Book IV, st. 17.

[14] Thomas Robinson, *The Life and Death of Mary Magdalene*, p. 10.

[15] *Ibid.*, p. 29.

[16] *Ibid.*, p. 31.

[17] *Ibid.*, p. 39.

[18] *Ibid.*, p. 46.

[19] *Ibid.*, p. 53.

[20] Joseph Beaumont, *The Complete Poems*, I, 76 f.

[21] *Ibid.*, p. 11.

[22] *Ibid.*, p. 13.

[23] *Ibid.*, p. 14.

[24] *Ibid.*, p. 16.

[25] *Ibid.*, pp. 22–23.

[26] *Ibid.*, p. 28.

[27] *Ibid.*, pp. 84–85.

[28] *Ibid.*, p. 119.

[29] See *ibid.*, Canto XVI, st. 103 f., for a discourse on the Tower of Babel and on languages.

[30] Edward Benlowes, *Theophila*, p. xvii.

NOTES TO CHAPTER V
(Pages 107–134)

[1] E. R. Curtius, *European Literature and the Latin Middle Ages*, p. 462.

[2] B. Rajan, *Paradise Lost and the Seventeenth Century Reader*, pp. 41–42.

[3] M. Y. Hughes, ed., *Paradise Lost*, pp. 4–5.

[4] The text for all quotations from Milton's poems is that of M. Y. Hughes (New York, 1935 and 1937).

[5] *The Works of John Milton* (Columbia Edition), XV, 273.

[6] H. J. C. Grierson, *Cross-Currents in English Literature* ... (1951), p. 285.

[7] R. J. Werblowsky's *Lucifer and Prometheus* is a study of Satan based upon Jungian principles.

[8] M. Y. Hughes, "The Christ of *Paradise Regained* and the Renaissance Heroic Tradition," *SP*, XXXV (1938), 254–277.

[9] *Ibid.*, p. 269.

[10] *Ibid.*, p. 264.

[11] *The Works of John Milton* (Columbia Edition), XVIII, 229–232.

[12] *Ibid.*, p. 232.

[13] Don Cameron Allen, *The Harmonious Vision*, p. 117.

[14] *Ibid.*, p. 119.

[15] Arnold Stein, *Heroic Knowledge*.

[16] Realizing that there are many questions concerning form and purpose which might be raised by introducing *Samson Agonistes* in a study of heroic narrative, I wish to suggest only that the theme of Christian heroism found in the tragedy is related to those of the heroic poems.

[17] M. Y. Hughes, ed., *Milton: Prose Selections*, pp. 223–224.

BIBLIOGRAPHY

BIBLIOGRAPHY

Primary Sources: The Biblical Narrative Poems

Alexander, Sir William. *Doomes-day, or The Great Day of the Lord's Judgment* (Edinburgh, 1614), and *Jonathan: An Heroicke Poeme Intended* (London, 1637), ed. L. E. Kastner and H. B. Charlton. Vol. XXIV (N.S.). Edinburgh: Scottish Text Society, 1929.

Aylett, Robert. *Joseph, or Pharaoh's Favorite*. London, 1623. University Microfilm Series, no. 17075. Ann Arbor, Michigan.

—— *Susanna, or the Morall Triall of the Unjust Elders*. London, 1622. Microfilm. Original in the Newberry Library.

Beaumont, Joseph. *Psyche, or Love's Mystery* (2d ed., London, 1702), in *The Complete Poems of Joseph Beaumont*, ed. A. B. Grosart. 2 vols. Chertsey Worthies' Library. Edinburgh, 1880.

Benlowes, Edward. *Theophila, or Love's Sacrifice*. London, 1652. Microfilm. Original in the William Andrews Clark Library.

Boyd, Zachary. *Four Poems from "Zion's Flowers,"* ed. Gabriel Neal. Glasgow, 1855.

Cowley, Abraham. *Davideis* (London, 1656), in *The Complete Works of Abraham Cowley*, ed. A. B. Grosart. Chertsey Worthies' Library. Edinburgh, 1881.

Crashaw, Richard. *The Suspicion of Herod* (London, 1646), in *The Poems*, ed. L. C. Martin. Oxford, 1927.

Drayton, Michael. *The Works of Michael Drayton*, ed. J. W. Hebel. 5 vols. Oxford, 1931–1941.

—— *David and Golia* (1630), in *The Works*.

—— *The Harmonie of the Churche* (1591). London: Percy Society, 1843.

—— *Moses His Birth and Miracles* (1604), in *The Works*.

—— *Noah's Flood* (1630), in *The Works*.

Du Bartas, William of Salust, Lord. *The Works of Guillaume De Salluste Sieur Du Bartas*, ed. U. T. Holmes, Jr., J. C. Lyons, R. W. Linker. 3 vols. Chapel Hill: University of North Carolina Press, 1935–1940.

Fletcher, Giles. *Christ's Victorie in Heaven and Earth, over, and after Death* (1610), in *The Complete Poems*, ed. A. B. Grosart. London, 1876.

Fletcher, Joseph. *The Perfect-Cursed-Blessed Man* (ca. 1629), in *The Poems of Joseph Fletcher*, ed. A. B. Grosart. The Fuller Worthies' Library. 1869.

Fletcher, Phineas. *The Apollyonists* (1627), in *The Poems of Phineas Fletcher*, ed. A. B. Grosart. Vol. II. The Fuller Worthies' Library. 1869.

Fuller, Thomas. *David's Heinous Sin, David's Hearty Repentance, David's Heavy Punishment* (1631), ed. William Nichols. London, 1867.

Hudson, Thomas. *The Historie of Judith* (1584), translated from the French of Du Bartas, ed. James Craigie. Series 3, Vol. XIV. Edinburgh: Scottish Text Society, 1941.

Hunnis, William. *A Hyve Full of Hunnye*. 1578. Microfilm. Original in the Huntington Library.

Lodge, Thomas. *A Learned Summarie upon the famous poeme of William of Salust, Lord of Bartas*. Printed for R. M., London, 1636.

Milton, John. *The Works of John Milton*, edited by various hands under the general editorship of Frank A. Patterson. Columbia Edition. 18 vols. New York, 1931–1938.

—— *Complete Prose Works of John Milton*, general editor Don M. Wolfe. Vol. I: *1624–1642*. New Haven: Yale University Press, 1953.

—— *Milton: Prose Selections*, ed. M. Y. Hughes. New York: Odyssey Press, 1947.

—— *Paradise Lost*, ed. M. Y. Hughes. New York: Odyssey Press, 1935.

————— *Paradise Regained,* ed. M. Y. Hughes. New York: Odyssey Press, 1937.

Munday, Anthony. *The Mirrour of Mutabilitie.* Imprinted by I. Allde, 1579. Microfilm. Original in the Huntington Library.

Mure, Sir William. *Doomesday: containing Hells horrour and Heavens happinesse* (1628), ed. William Tough. Vol. XL. Edinburgh: Scottish Text Society, 1898.

Peyton, Thomas. *The Glasse of Time in the First Age* (1620); *The Glasse of Time in the Second Age* (1623). Reprinted by John B. Alden. New York, 1886.

Quarles, Francis. *The Works of Francis Quarles,* ed. A. B. Grosart. Vol. II. Chertsey Worthies' Library. Edinburgh, 1880.

————— *A Feast for Wormes set forth in a Poeme of the History of Jonah* (London, 1626), in *The Works.*

————— *Hadassa, or the History of Queene Ester* (London, 1621), in *The Works.*

————— *The Historie of Samson* (London, 1631), in *The Works.*

————— *Job Militant* (London, 1624), in *The Works.*

Robinson, Thomas. *The Life and Death of Mary Magdalene (ca.* 1620), ed. H. O. Sommer. Series 2, no. 78. London: Early English Text Society, 1899.

Sabie, Francis. *Adam's Complaint, The Olde Worlde's Tragedie, David and Bethsabe.* London, 1596. University Microfilm Series, no. 15401. Ann Arbor, Michigan.

Sandys, George. *A Paraphrase upon Job* (1638), ed. Richard Hooper. Vol. I. London, 1872.

Sylvester, Joshuah, trans. *The Divine Workes and Weekes of Du Bartas* (Folio of 1641), ed. A. B. Grosart. 2 vols. Chertsey Worthies' Library. Edinburgh, 1880.

————— *Job Triumphant in His Triall,* in *The Divine Workes.* Vol. II.

————— *The Maiden's Blush; or Joseph, Mirror of Modestie, Map of Pietie, Maze of Destinie, Or rather, Divine Providence,* translated from the Latin of Jerome Fracaster, in *The Divine Workes.* Vol. II.

Secondary Sources

Adams, Robert M. *Ikon: John Milton and the Modern Critics.* Ithaca: Cornell University Press, 1955.

Allen, Don Cameron. *The Harmonious Vision: Studies in Milton's Poetry.* Baltimore: Johns Hopkins Press, 1954.

————— *The Legend of Noah; Renaissance Rationalism in Art, Science and Letters.* Illinois Studies in Language and Literature, vol. 33, nos. 3–4 (1949).

Auden, W. H. *The Enchafèd Flood.* New York: Random House, 1950.

Auerbach, Erich. *Mimesis: The Representation of Reality in Western Literature,* translated from the German by Willard R. Trask. Princeton: Princeton University Press, 1953.

Augustine, Saint. *The City of God* (1610 edition), translated by John Healy. 2 vols. Edinburgh, 1909.

Aulén, Gustaf. *Christus Victor,* translated by A. G. Hebert. New York: The Macmillan Co., 1954.

Baroway, Israel. "The Bible as Poetry in the English Renaissance: An Introduction," *JEGP,* XXXII (1933), 447–480.

Bloomfield, M. W. *The Seven Deadly Sins.* East Lansing: Michigan State College Press, 1952.

Bowra, C. M. *From Virgil to Milton.* London: Macmillan and Co., Ltd., 1948.

————— *Heroic Poetry.* London: Macmillan and Co., Ltd., 1952.

Bush, Douglas. *English Literature in the Earlier Seventeenth Century.* Oxford: Clarendon Press, 1945.

———— *Paradise Lost in Our Time.* New York: P. Smith, 1948.

———— *The Renaissance and English Humanism.* Toronto: University of Toronto Press, 1939.

Campbell, Lily B. "The Christian Muse," *Huntington Library Bulletin,* no. 8 (October, 1935), 29–70.

Carmelite Brothers, sponsors. *Satan.* New York: Sheed and Ward, 1952.

Cruttwell, Patrick. *The Shakespearean Moment.* London: Chatto and Windus, 1954.

Curtius, E. R. *European Literature and the Latin Middle Ages,* translated by Willard R. Trask. Bollingen Series, Vol. XXXVI. New York: Pantheon Books, Inc., 1953.

Farrell, Thomas, Jr. *The Classical Biblical Epic in England.* Unpublished dissertation, University of Iowa, 1950.

Frank, R. W., Jr. "The Art of Reading Medieval Personification Allegory," *ELH,* XX (December, 1953), 237–250.

Frye, Northrup. "The Typology of *Paradise Regained,"* *MP,* LIII, 227–238.

Goodspeed, E. J. *A History of Early Christian Literature.* Chicago: University of Chicago Press, 1942.

Grierson, H. J. C. *Cross-Currents in English Literature of the Seventeenth Century.* London, 1929.

———— *Milton and Wordsworth: Poets and Prophets.* Cambridge, England, 1937.

Haller, William. *The Rise of Puritanism.* New York: Columbia University Press, 1938.

Hamilton, G. R. *Hero or Fool? A Study of Milton's Satan.* London: G. Allen and Unwin, Ltd., 1944.

Hughes, M. Y. "The Christ of *Paradise Regained* and the Renaissance Heroic Tradition," *SP,* XXXV (1938), 254–277.

Jenkins, Harold. *Edward Benlowes.* Cambridge, Mass.: Harvard University Press, 1952.

Johnson, Samuel. *The Life of Milton,* in *The Lives of the English Poets.* London, 1779–1781.

Jonas, Leah. *The Divine Science.* New York: Columbia University Press, 1940.

Jones, Charles W. "Milton's 'Brief Epic,'" *SP,* XLIV (1947), 209–227.

Kermode, Frank. "Milton's Hero," *RES,* IV (N. S.), 317–330.

Kirkconnell, Watson. *The Celestial Cycle.* Toronto: University of Toronto Press, 1952.

Krouse, F. M. *Milton's Samson and the Christian Tradition.* Princeton: Princeton University Press, 1949.

Lewis, C. S. *Preface to Paradise Lost.* London: Oxford University Press, 1942.

Loiseau, Jean. *Abraham Cowley, Sa Vie, Son Oeuvre.* Paris, 1931.

Lovejoy, A. O. "Milton and the Paradox of the Fortunate Fall," in *Essays in the History of Ideas.* Baltimore: Johns Hopkins Press, 1948.

McBryde, J. M., Jr. "A Study of Cowley's *Davideis,"* *JGP,* II, no. 4 (1898), 454–527.

McColley, Grant. *Paradise Lost.* Chicago: Packard and Co., 1940.

Mahood, M. M. *Poetry and Humanism.* London: Jonathan Cape, 1950.

Marni, Archimede. *Allegory in the French Heroic Poem of the Seventeenth Century.* Princeton: Princeton University Press, 1936.

Miles, Josephine. "The Sublime Poem," in *The Image of the Work: Essays in Criticism.* University of California Publications in English, vol. 11 (1955).

Nethercot, A. H. *Abraham Cowley: The Muses' Hannibal.* London, 1931.

Padelford, F. M. "Robert Aylett," *Huntington Library Bulletin,* no. 9 (October, 1936), 1–48.

Pope, Elizabeth M. *Paradise Regained: The Tradition and the Poem.* Baltimore: Johns Hopkins Press, 1947.

Puttenham, George. *The Arte of English Poesie,* ed. E. Arber. London, 1869.

Raby, F. J. E. *A History of Christian-Latin Poetry.* Oxford, 1927.

Rajan, B. *Paradise Lost and the Seventeenth Century Reader*. London: Oxford University Press, 1947.

Raleigh, Sir Walter. *The History of the World*. London, 1687.

Robbins, F. E. *The Hexameral Literature*. Chicago, 1912.

Sayce, R. A. *The French Biblical Epic in the Seventeenth Century*. London: Oxford University Press, 1955.

Schultz, Howard. *Milton and Forbidden Knowledge*. Revolving Fund Series. New York: Modern Language Association of America, 1955.

Smalley, Beryl. *The Study of the Bible in the Middle Ages*. Cambridge, England, 1941.

Smith, G. G. *Elizabethan Critical Essays*. 2 vols. Oxford, 1904.

Spingarn, J. E., ed. *Critical Essays of the Seventeenth Century*. 3 vols. Oxford, 1908.

Steele, Richard. "The Christian Hero," in *Tracts and Pamphlets by Richard Steele*, ed. R. Blanchard. Baltimore: Johns Hopkins Press, 1944.

Stein, Arnold. *Answerable Style*. Minneapolis: University of Minnesota Press, 1953.

——— *Heroic Knowledge*. Minneapolis: University of Minnesota Press, 1957.

Summers, J. H. *George Herbert: His Religion and Art*. Cambridge, Mass.: Harvard University Press, 1954.

Swedenberg, H. T., Jr. *The Theory of the Epic in England, 1650–1800*. University of California Publications in English, vol. 15 (1944).

Taylor, G. C. *Milton's Use of Du Bartas*. Cambridge, Mass.: Harvard University Press, 1934.

Thorpe, James, ed. *Milton Criticism*. New York: Rinehart and Co., Inc., 1950.

Tillyard, E. M. W. *The English Epic and Its Background*. New York: Oxford University Press, 1954.

——— *The Miltonic Setting, Past and Present*. Cambridge, England, 1939.

——— *Studies in Milton*. London: Chatto and Windus, 1951.

Tuve, Rosemond. *A Reading of George Herbert*. Chicago: University of Chicago Press, 1952.

Tuveson, Ernest L. *Millennium and Utopia: A Study in the Background of the Idea of Progress*. Berkeley and Los Angeles: University of California Press, 1949.

Vida, Marco Girolamo. *The Christiad*, translated by J. Cranwell. London, 1768.

Wallerstein, Ruth. *Studies in Seventeenth Century Poetic*. Madison: University of Wisconsin Press, 1950.

Werblowsky, R. J. *Lucifer and Prometheus: A Study of Milton's Satan*. London: Rutledge and Kegan Paul, 1952.

White, Helen C. *English Devotional Literature (Prose), 1600–1640*. University of Wisconsin Studies in Language and Literature, no. 29 (1931).

Whiting, G. W. *Milton's Literary Milieu*. Chapel Hill: University of North Carolina Press, 1939.

Willey, Basil. *The Seventeenth Century Background*. New York: Columbia University Press, 1950.

Williams, Arnold. *The Common Expositor: An Account of the Commentaries on Genesis*. Chapel Hill: University of North Carolina Press, 1948.